Dust

Dust

Kevin Marsh

Offspin
2015

First published in Great Britain by OffspinMedia in 2015

Copyright © 2015 by Kevin Marsh

All rights reserved.

The moral right of the author has been asserted.

ISBN 978-1-326-13048-0

This book or any portion thereof may not be reproduced or used in any manner whatsoever without the express written permission of the publisher except for the use of brief quotations in a book review or scholarly journal.

First Printing: 2015

It is sincerely believed that copyright has expired on all images (photographs and maps) that are not the work of the author.

Specifically, the photographs on pages 26, 27, 28, 29, 32, 33, 38, 83 and 131 and the maps on the following pages and on pp 55, 56, 103, 130, 142.

Any person who believes their copyright might have been infringed should contact the publisher at offspinmediauk@gmail.com

OffspinMedia Ltd
69 Lissenden Mansions
London NW5 1PR

www.offspinmedia.co.uk

'a richer dust concealed'

*Northern France in the early part of the Great War.
In the summer of 1915, the British sector stretched from
a little north of Ypres to La Bassée.
The line was extended to Loos in the autumn of 1915 and
further south in 1916.
'British' included units from the Empire and Dominions -
in particular India, Canada and Australia.*

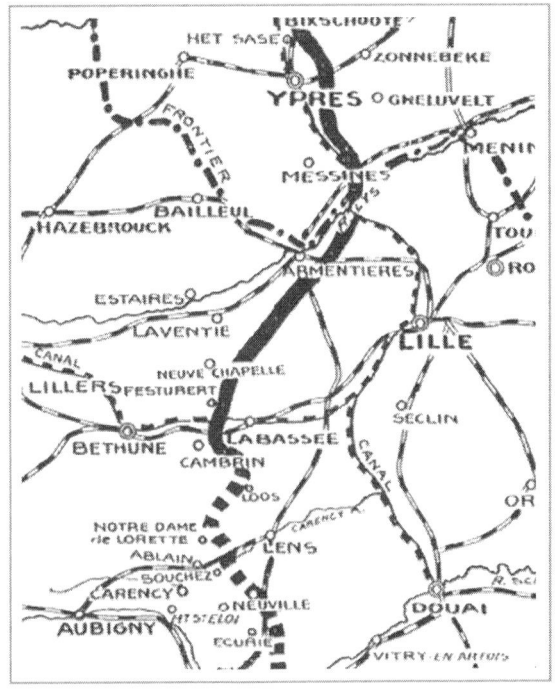

Detail of the British line at the end of summer 1915. By 25 September 1915, the British Expeditionary Force had extended its line to the ground west of the mining town of Loos.

Contents

Prologue	1
From Yorkshire to Hampshire	15
France	25
Billets	61
Plans	85
Trenches	97
Saturday 25 September 1915	147
Epilogue	171

Prologue

James Airton died on 25 September 1915. Probably in the morning, probably around seven o'clock. Perhaps a little before. No-one now knows exactly when. Or exactly where. Or exactly how. A handful of men might have known once. But what they knew, if they knew anything, is lost.

He has no grave. Nothing of the man remains. Not even memory. Not living memory. No-one alive can tell you what his voice sounded like. How he moved. His manners and moods. His likes and dislikes. His weaknesses and failings. His hopes and his sadnesses.

He is a name chiseled into a limestone wall. He is a single photograph. He is three postcards. That is all. Almost all. Even officialdom's eyes that looked ever more closely into 20th century lives focused seldom on Jim. There is a birth and a marriage. Then another birth, that of his son.

Twice he appears on the nation's roll-call. The census. Once misspelt. And we can infer where he lived as a boy. Perhaps where he went to school. A little of the life of his family and the character of his father. And there is a death.

We can infer. Nothing more.

Three bent and frayed pieces of card tell something of his life. Five fragile pieces of paper, each almost dust, tell something of his death.

James - Jim - was a soldier. A Lance Corporal. He died in the infantry assault at the Battle of Loos. He was twenty four years old.

Before he was a soldier, he was a miner. Born in the West Riding of Yorkshire, in Doncaster, to a family from the North and East Ridings. He was a husband. May Alberta's husband. Father to their boy, also called James. 'Little James'.

Jim. Miner and soldier.

And son. His father was constantly on the move in the 1890s and 1900s. Looking for work. He found it in a shop. In a pub. Laboured in the mines by Mansfield in Nottinghamshire. Always moving. Place to place. Job to job. It kept him and his family from the workhouse. Paid their way but never with much to spare. And for some reason he would tell officials he had been born in 'California, Yorkshire'.

He was actually born near Bridlington on the Yorkshire coast.

We know that Jim was one of 12 children. The fifth. And that he was born in March 1891 in a tiny house - four rooms - in a pub yard. No 14 Cheshire Cheese Yard on the south-eastern fringe of Doncaster town centre. His father was cellarman there. It was not the best job nor the best part of town. By the sewage works and town gas plant. On the edge of the River Don's flood plain.

The pub still stands. Just. A road scheme that meant to flatten it in the early 21st century skirted by it in the end.

Around the turn of the 20th century, the family left their small house in the Cheshire Cheese yard

May Johnson, soon to become May Airton, photographed in about 1912.

and moved but not very far. To a row of houses facing the pub, a row called 'The Holmes'. They were slums. They do not survive. Another house, though, does. No 3 Milbanke Street. A tiny house.

James Airton, photographed soon after joining the 6th King's Own Scottish Borderers. He does not yet carry the stripes of a Lance Corporal

Tinier than the rows of terraced houses that were springing up elsewhere in the town in the last years of the 19th century.

A few years later, they moved to Mansfield in Nottinghamshire and work in the pits. Jim's father and, perhaps a few years after the move, Jim too.

The 20 year old Jim is invisible to the 1911 census. Invisible to history until he and May Alberta Johnson married on Sunday 5 July 1914 at St James' Church in Doncaster. A grimy limestone heap close to the station and the main London to Edinburgh railway line. A church designed "for utility rather than ornament". Its architect believed it to be "the exact climax of pure gothic". We do not know how well he understood irony.

We know nothing of Jim and May's first meeting. How long or where they courted. What their wedding day was like. We do know, however, that seven days before that wedding, the event took place that was the first tug on the many threads drawing Jim to his death.

The assassination of the heir presumptive to the Austro-Hungarian throne, the Archduke Franz Ferdinand of Austria. What some modern historians call Austria's '9/11 moment'. An act of terror that fired fear and anger in a great empire, Austria.

The assassin was Bosnian. A subject of the Austro-Hungarian empire. But his nationality was Serbian and he saw himself, as did the others in the assassination plot, as a pan-Slav nationalist. On the side of history, fighting for a free, united Yugoslavia.

But as far as Vienna was concerned it was an act of terror. Serbia, an independent Slav kingdom on its south eastern border, had to pay for these pan-Slav aspirations.

Even if May and Jim and their wedding guests had been aware of that event – perhaps they were; it was front page news – they could not have known what it would mean. No-one did.

It was high summer. Those who could took holidays. No-one could have thought that within a month of Jim and May's wedding, Britain would have shambled into an unwanted continental European war. That within two, Jim would be in uniform. And that within fifteen, he would be dead.

Dust. A lifeless miner lost in a field amongst the coal pits of northern France.

Now, today, we can stand in that field perhaps at the place Jim died. Perhaps close to it. We can never know how close. But under a bright April sky we can deceive ourselves that we can see in these neat fields and early shoots of rape and beans and sugar beet that dank autumn dawn of ninety-nine years before.

We cannot.

We know the story too well. Or think we do. We know it too little, in fact. We steer a way around hard blocks of half truths. We know too little to shift them aside.

We play and replay a handful of images that we call 'The Great War'.

We do not know 'The Great War'. We know nothing, can know nothing of what was or might have been in the minds and lives of those who did not know, as we do, what was to come.

Nor can we begin to think or believe that all that we now know was, did not have to be.

***

In one of the world's oldest languages, the way you say 'the past' is almost the same as the way you say 'to face something'. To them, to those who spoke and thought in that oldest of languages there was no other way of thinking other than that we walk backwards through our presents. Facing our pasts not our futures.

Facing our pasts because we see each fleeting present only inside the shape of all that we can know. From our pasts.

Our pasts mock us. History mocks us. Not like friends mock. Gently, meaning to share the joke when it's done. Not even like our enemies mock us, meaning to hurt.

It mocks us with indifference. It is irony. It does not care that we stumble backwards into our futures. Not knowing how our hopes and plans and wishes that make sense in our pasts make none in our futures.

***

It is unlikely that May and Jim followed closely the Balkan crisis of July 1914. The crisis that turned into a European and, eventually, British crisis. They cannot have known that on the day of their wedding, Germany's Kaiser Wilhelm handed what became known as the 'blank cheque' to his Austro-Hungarian allies. The promise of unconditional support for whatever it was that its ally wanted to do to Serbia. Even if it meant war with Serbia's ally, Russia. And … and … and.

We know now, but it was much less clear then, that this was the decisive twist to that thread of events that turned petulant Viennese threats against an obscure Balkan kingdom into a European and then world war.

Historians will argue for as long as anyone still cares whether the Great War was avoidable. Avoidable for Britain. A chunk of Asquith's cabinet certainly thought it was. By some calculations, eleven of the nineteen ministers opposed war. Four resigned, though two later returned to the cabinet table. After all, the start of the 20th century had seen one Balkan War after another that had done no-one in Britain any harm. And while we might have obligations to France, the 'Entente Cordiale' stopped short of an explicit military alliance. Except that the Foreign Secretary, Sir Edward Grey, had quietly – secretly – deepened and strengthened that entente until it was indistinguishable from an alliance proper. With all the obligations that entailed.

Germany's ultimatum to neutral Belgium on 1 August and Belgium's rejection two days later became the narrative that swung public opinion behind war. And the inevitability that Britain would have to join it.

Even so, on 3 August, the eve of war, many Liberal MPs, members of the governing party, secured a debate in parliament where they argued forcefully that a European war was no business of Britain. They did not trust Sir Edward Grey. But then, he did not trust them and thought foreign affairs were nothing to do with the House of Commons.

Sir Edward had held his nose and delivered a statement to the House that afternoon. Setting out his and the Prime Minister's case for war. Opposition was muted at first. But feeling festered and late that evening, recalcitrant MPs persuaded the Speaker to grant a short adjournment debate. One MP after another rose to his feet to condemn the government and shout their suspicion that Sir Edward had not told them the whole truth. They believed he had made a secret deal that was bundling the nation into a war that would destroy

British commerce for a generation. A few feared it would destroy a generation, too.

It is a hard idea for us to hold now. That one of the defining episodes in the national memory might never have been.

What is beyond argument is that the Battle of Loos, the battle in which Jim died, was avoidable. More. It was unwanted. Unwanted by the generals who had begun to understand the new science of trench warfare. That it was a type of war that gave overwhelming advantage to the defenders. That attack demanded the sacrifice of thousands of men and tons of munitions that Britain did not have, could not produce and could not afford to lose.

Winning that battle would have meant driving the Germans out of some of their strongest positions on the Western Front. It never made military sense. But the generals had to plan for it and the men had to die in it for the sake of politics and diplomacy. To fulfil the demands and realise, fail to realise, the dreams of French generals.

Loos was one part of the biggest land battle to date in modern European history. Bigger were to come. But on that September dawn, the British generals, watching from their observation towers knew that even if the day went well, thousands would die. The ground was suicidal; they had said so. They had not the men and the munitions; they had said so. And they were experimenting with a chemical weapon, chlorine gas, they had never used before against an enemy that had dug and cemented itself into semi-subterranean fortresses.

It was the weave of these threads, the decisions of men and not the fabric of fate, that pulled Jim to France.

To Loos. To his death.

From Yorkshire to Hampshire

We know almost nothing of James Airton's childhood, of his teenage years nor of his life as a young man. We do not know where he went to school. Whether he was a good and conscientious scholar. We know he could read and write – or at least, that he could form copperplate letters that said something. Not all children of his generation got that far.

We do not know how old he was when he left school. Whether, like many children of the time, he started working while still going to lessons. We can infer that his home life was tough. The houses he and his family lived in were more than small. They were tiny. Matchboxes. And if his father's work gave the family the greater part of its income, money was tight.

We do not know whether his was a loving family in spite of the hardship we can infer. Whether Jim was well or badly behaved. Whether he got into more fights than most young men. Whether he was honest. Sober. Religious. We know nothing of his ambitions or his hopes. And we do not know how, where or when he met his future wife. May Alberta Johnson.

May was, like Jim, a child of a large family. Her mother, Ellen, brought fourteen children into the world. Twelve survived. May was the tenth, born in 1896. Her father, Arthur, was a builder. Born near Spalding in Lincolnshire, he'd made his living throwing up ribbon rows of cheap brick houses in Doncaster and around. Homes for pitmen, railwaymen, factory hands and their families.

By the time May was in her teens, she and her family were living in three linked houses her father had built around a courtyard and stables. A Johnson compound. The houses were bigger and of a significantly better quality than the terraces in the rest of the street.

In the front room of one of the houses, her parents had opened a grocery and sweet shop. The young children worked there. In the stables and yard behind the houses Arthur kept his carts and dray horses and burnt the rubbish from the shop.

In the three linked houses at various times and in various combinations lived May's grown-up brothers, married sisters and – in due course – her fiancé and then husband, Jim.

The photographs of the family that survive are strong evidence that Arthur and his children saw themselves firmly within the Victorian/Edwardian ideal. Proud. Self-reliant. Thrifty. Moral. Patriotic. And a tiny bit Christian.

We do not know how James Airton, miner and miner's son, came into the world of May Johnson, builder's and shopkeeper's daughter. Perhaps Jim worked as a labourer on one of Arthur's building gangs. Many young men did.

Eight of the Johnsons pictured outside the 'compound', in about 1910. May is fourth from the right.

Perhaps he met May in the stable yard at the end of a working day. Or perhaps he came to know May's brothers first. Two of them lived in the Johnson compound, in the house next door to May and their parents. They were 'pit sinkers'. A skilled,

*Two Johnsons pictured outside the shop window.
Probably 1910.*

dangerous, filthy job. Digging hundreds of feet down into the earth, through sodden sandstone to the coal seams under Bentley, Brodsworth, Maltby, Edlington and Rossington. Perhaps Jim met one or both brothers at the mine where he worked. He certainly knew them. At the time of his wedding to May, he was living with them.

No account survives of Jim and May's short married life. Except that they conceived their son, also called James, within weeks of their wedding. Little James – he was always called that to distinguish him from his father – was born on 23 April 1915. By then, his father was already a Lance Corporal in the 6th Battalion of the King's Own Scottish Borderers, training in Hampshire. Three weeks later, he would set foot in France for the first time.

Jim was one of the 'first hundred thousand' who'd charged the recruitment offices in August and September 1914. The first tenth of the million men some in government and more in the Army predicted would be needed for a war that would not be over by Christmas. Not Christmas 1914 at any rate.

We do not know exactly when, exactly where or exactly why he joined. His military records were amongst the millions destroyed in the Second World War. Most intriguing of all, we do not know whether he knew that May was pregnant with their first child when he signed the papers committing to the

Borderers 'for three years or the duration of the war'.

It is at least possible that in August or September of 1914, May herself could not have been sure her and Jim's child was already within her. And we have to wonder when or how she told her husband. Whether there there were tears for misplaced time. Resentment. Or the stoicism that we see in the faces of the Johnson clan in every family photograph.

The battalion Jim joined was one of the first units of the 'new armies'. 'K1' that first new army was called. Kitchener One, after the War Secretary, Lord Kitchener, who led the recruitment drive.

Why Jim joined the Borderers rather than one of the Yorkshire regiments is, like so much, unknown now. Englishmen from Cumbria and Northumbria were not uncommon in the regiment. Jim's father had family in Teesdale. Not quite the borders. But perhaps there was a connection there.

In spite of the Englishmen in the Borderers' ranks, the English regiments called them all 'Jocks'. It was what they called every Scottish unit. In truth, the Borderers had a divided personality. Their uniforms were the least emphatically Scottish. No kilts or sporrans. But they did wear Tam o' Shanters, tartan banded forage caps and discreet Scots insignia. And were unambiguously Scots in tradition and ethos. They were, for example, piped into battle.

Jim's battalion, the sixth, was raised in Berwick. As 'borderer' a town as you can get. Straddling the Tweed. Its north in Scotland, its south in England. In the autumn of 1914 they began their training in Hampshire. First in Bordon and then, from March 1915, Bramshott. Camps that were sprawling masses of barracks, tents and parade grounds close to Aldershot. The territorials and reservists had been refreshing their fighting skills there from the moment war became inevitable.

Many in that first 'hundred thousand', the first volunteers, showed extraordinary physical fitness. A condition not guaranteed in young working class men in 1914 when malnutrition and cramped, insanitary housing led to startling physical differences between them and the middle classes - a difference in height of three or four inches was not uncommon. Those first volunteers were above average in education, too, and, unsurprisingly, had fierce patriotic motivation.

Physical fitness, intelligence and resourcefulness were all needed at Bordon and Bramshott. At first, many had to drill without arms or uniforms. March without military boots. And, more significantly, learn to shoot, throw bombs and understand the basics of tactics and strategy without instructors with any recent experience of warfare. Certainly no experience of the kind of semi-subterranean, defensive warfare that was taking shape on the Western Front. In the camps, there was endless marching, saluting, marching, PT, marching, more marching and then some more marching.

The 6th King's Own Scottish Borderers came under the orders of the 28th Infantry Brigade. Shortly before their deployment to France, they transferred to the 27th Brigade to join the 11th and 12th Royal Scots and the 9th Cameronians, the Scottish Rifles. That Infantry Brigade, along with the 26th Highland Infantry Brigade, the South African Infantry Brigade and the 9th (Service) Battalion of the Seaforth Highlanders, formed the 9th (Scottish) Division, the senior 'Kitchener' division.

Jim and his battalion trained in Hampshire for nine months. Longer than the six that was the recommended minimum. Much longer than the few weeks that became the norm later in the war.

During those nine months, he had few chances to take leave and travel to Yorkshire to see his pregnant wife. But in late April or early May 1915, he will have been able to see his boy of a few weeks. It was usual for men to be granted 10 or 14 days leave immediately before they embarked for France.

France

Jim's battalion left Hampshire for France on Wednesday 12 May 1915.

Whatever his education or talent for war, one or both evidently marked him out. He went to France, not as a private but as a Lance Corporal, the most junior rank of the battalion's non-commissioned officers. Traditionally, the Lance Corporal was the 'go to' man in a platoon or section and in 1914/15 could take on one of many duties; command of a section, usually about 12 men, if a Corporal was absent, wounded or killed; or he could be a specialist of some kind – a machine-gunner, for example. They were often casually appointed and sometimes

The SS Invicta, pictured leaving Folkestone in 1913

unpaid. Day to day, they were the men's first point of contact with the command of their section and platoon. From a letter that May wrote to the War Office in autumn 1915, we know that Jim was in 15th platoon, D company, of the 6th KOSB. From his battalion's war diaries we know that he was probably one of the 857 men under the command of 26 Officers who marched from Bramshott in Hampshire to Liphook station at 2 pm on that Wednesday afternoon. The first short march on their journey to the Western Front.

Boulogne, pictured just before the war. Thousands of British soldiers marched over this bridge over the Liane

By 4 pm they were on board two trains that took them to Folkestone where they arrived four hours later. Almost immediately, at 8.30 pm, they embarked on the SS Invicta which sailed a mere ten minutes later. The previous day, the Invicta had

*Pont de Briques. Top: the road outside the station.
Bottom: the Grand Place.*

carried the regimental transport – 3 officers, 106 men, 78 horses and 24 vehicles – from Southampton to Le Havre. It is possible, of course, that Jim was in this group rather than the main body of the battalion. But we know nothing now of any specialism he might have had.

Pont de Briques. Top: the railway station. Bottom: Rue de l'Eglise

That night, there was fog in the channel. Some of the ferries pressed into service as troop ships were delayed. It seems the Invicta was not. It took two hours and twenty minutes to make the crossing to Boulogne. The battalion arrived at 11 pm. It's not recorded how or where the men spent the night, but

29

at 9.30 the following morning they paraded in heavy rain and marched to Pont de Briques, a village by a railway yard on the southern outskirts of Boulogne.

The 6th KOSB was not the only battalion passing through Pont de Briques in mid-May. The Grand Place, with its café and estaminet, saw thousands of British troops muster before they embarked on trains at the small station or the larger sidings nearby. The Borderers' train took them to St Omer where they arrived at 2 pm and marched from there the few miles west to billets in Tatinghem. Another village swamped by the thousands of troops passing through who would spend nights in the countryside around, a landscape which was rapidly turning into a near-replica of Hampshire. Camps and training areas sprang up all over the low-rolling land. The battalion stayed at or close to Tatinghem for just two days before moving, on 16 May, to Oxelaere - before the war, a quiet agricultural village below one of the few real hills in the northern countryside - and the following day to Outtersteene, a small town that was little more than a bleak crossroads .

It's not known whether the battalion's officers knew where in the British line they were to be deployed first. In mid-May, that line was just over 30 miles long and stretched from the La BasséeLa Bassée canal – properly called the Canal d'Aire – in the south to Bixschoote, north-east of Ypres, in the north. Much of the line was, by May 1915, static and relatively "quiet". But towards the south, near Aubers, Richebourg and Festubert, fighting had recently been fierce and was soon to be again.

***

While Jim and his battalion were moving billets from Tatinghem to Oxelaere and Outtestreete, the opening bombardment of what became known as the Battle of Festubert was under way. The continuation of an earlier battle, the Battle of Aubers Ridge.

That earlier battle, on 9 May 1915, was a murderous fiasco. Eleven thousand British soldiers were killed or wounded for no gain. The later Battle of Festubert began on 13 May with a 60 hour artillery bombardment. British gunners rained over 100,000 shells on the German trenches that first night. The infantry attacked on 15/16 May, the first British night attack of the war. By 25 May when the

Oxelaere

battle petered out, 16,000 men were dead or wounded. They and those who survived had won a strip of land a few yards wide.

When Jim and his battalion finally entered the front line trenches in earnest, it would be to defend

Outtersteene

this strip of land. But that was six weeks in the future. On the night of 13 May, that narrow strip was not yet won.

We cannot know their thoughts and feelings on that first night in billets in the French countryside. Jim and his battalion would have heard the sound of the heavy guns at Festubert, some 30 miles away. There would have been excitement. Apprehension, perhaps. Certainly the sense that this was now for real. The battles they'd been preparing for were now close. Few slept. Their surroundings were alien. Almost all had never left Scotland or England before. And those who did not sleep felt the angry rumble over the horizon. Watched the damp night sky burst into unnatural daylight.

***

These battles of May 1915, Aubers Ridge and Festubert, were the British contribution to a French grand plan to push the Germans out of Artois and Champagne. That would be the grand plan in the autumn, too. At Loos.

It's not difficult to understand French insistence and urgency in wanting to drive German troops off French soil. Their presence was at best a grotesque national insult at worst an existential threat. Every French man and woman over the age of 50 could remember the fall of Paris to German invaders in 1871. Unsurprisingly, the French military chiefs Joffre and Foch were determined to end that insult, lift the threat to France's existence and avert a repetition of that humiliation. No British general would argue with that. But there was an important difference of perspective between the French and the British.

For Britain, the war was one of political choice. Quite how that choice came to be made, quite how much deception there was at the highest level remains an open question. But what is certainly the case is that German violation of Belgian neutrality and its armies' rapid advances in the direction of Paris presented Britain with no existential threat. The 85,000 regulars and reservists of the original British Expeditionary Force went to France that sultry summer to contain and defend. To halt Germany in its tracks. Frustrate their march on Paris. Fulfil the terms of an ill-defined entente, a duplicitous alliance.

It was a close run thing. And the cost in blood was enormous – by the turn of 1914, the number of British casualties exceeded the size of the original expeditionary force. But defence was always uppermost in the British military mind - with the exception of the handful of the most senior who still dreamed of battles settled by dragoons, charging the enemy on horseback. And the precedence of defence was underlined in the war's early battles. During and after the First Battle of Ypres in October 1914, the clearest military minds realised that this new, accidental form of warfare - trench warfare - would define the conflict.

Swift attacks could win a brief advantage. Pierce the defenders' line. Capture briefly a few yards of enemy trench. But the essence of this war would be a mutual siege. Not of a city or single location. But at every point along the line that stretched from the English Channel to the Swiss frontier.

Along the whole of that front, hundreds of thousands of troops faced one another. Well dug in. In most places, neither presented a flank to the enemy. Behind, heavy artillery and the roads and railways that could speed men, rations and reinforcements to the front - as well as munitions, though they were always in short supply on the British side.

One of the men who had most to learn about this new form of warfare was General Douglas Haig. He was the senior officer in command of one half of the

British Expeditionary Force. The First Army or 1 Corps. Jim's battalion was one small part of that army.

Most of those who came across Haig judged him to be intellectually sharp and clear-sighted, a superb administrator but an appalling public speaker. He was a veteran of the Sudan and Boer Wars and had held a senior post in the cavalry in India. There, his conservative side had come out. He was one of a dwindling number of senior officers who argued that the cavalry should still be drilled in charging on horseback, armed with sabre and lance.

While a young officer, Haig became close to the man who was to become the Commander in Chief of the British Expeditionary Force - John French, later Sir John French. That closeness is said to have derived from an occasion when Haig saved John French's career, lending him the cash to save his commission when he lost a fortune on unwise investments.

Over time, though, it became a strained relationship. Haig's rise was rapid - he became the youngest Major General in the British Army - and his intellectual superiority over French was striking.

Clockwise from top left: General Haig, Sir John French, General Joffre, General Foch

During the first year of the war, the two were proximate rather than close. Their dealings with each other marked by mutual suspicion and, eventually, hostility.

One of the unresolved puzzles of the first year of war is why Haig failed to turn his intellectual capabilities into military reality. Contrary to many claims made about him, he was not a stubborn man, indifferent to the fate of the men he commanded. Not at first, anyway. It is the case, though, that by July 1916 he felt comfortable describing the loss of 40,000 men in one day - the casualty estimate on the first day of the Battle of the Somme - as a number that "cannot be considered severe in view of the numbers engaged and the length of front attacked".

As early as 1909, he'd foreseen that war with Germany was inevitable. And on the eve of that war, he predicted it would be long, attritional and costly in human life.

It is clear that Haig and his senior officers understood the lessons of the first months of war - they discussed them often enough and recorded those discussions in diaries and memos. It is just as clear he and they failed to apply them. One in particular. In spite of Haig's "grave doubts" about the temper and military abilities of French generals, he allowed himself to be manoeuvred into positions where he was required to do their bidding. And while he had a distaste for self-serving politicians, he found himself unable to prevent them calling his shots.

***

Aubers Ridge was a fiasco. Festubert a debacle. Both bloody, sacrificial beyond anything we can imagine today. And both were doomed to failure precisely because of that huge disparity between attack and defence in this new style of static war. But both were fought - as would Loos be in the autumn of 1915 - because the politics of alliance demanded it.

By the spring of 1915, Germany's original war plan – to knock France out quickly so that it could focus all its efforts on Russia, the enemy whose power it truly feared – was turned on its head. In the west, there was stalemate. Neither side able to deliver the knockout blow. In the east, Russia was faltering. The French generals feared that if Russia were knocked out, Germany could turn its attention to the west.

Not for the last time, France demanded a 'big push'. To take the pressure off Russia. Exactly the kind of offensive that sensible military minds now doubted could ever be successful without overwhelming superiority in both men and guns.

The French Commander in Chief General Joffre proposed that:

> *"In the last days of April, the French Tenth Army, acting in concert with the British First Army, will undertake an important attack north of Arras with a view to piercing the enemy's line."*

Joffre hoped the attack would not only take the pressure off Russia, he dreamed it might even drive German troops from French soil. Or at least, significantly back in the general direction of Berlin.

As it turned out, the 'important attack' was a mess even before it was launched. First it was postponed until the end of the first week of May. Then it had to be changed at the last minute from a phased attack into a single one. In the original plan, the French were to mount an assault on Vimy Ridge first. The British to mount theirs later, near Aubers. But there was heavy rain and fog on the dates planned for the French attacks, so they were cancelled. On 9 May, all went ahead together.

The ground the British faced at Aubers was difficult. In places, impossible. It was and is very flat. The only outstanding feature the barely perceptible rise that is Aubers Ridge. That was held by German troops. When the British infantry advanced, they had no natural cover and had to wade their way over what was in places a bog deeply gouged with drainage ditches ten or fifteen feet wide.

The German trenches had been exceptionally well prepared and strengthened. They were more or less untouched by a British artillery bombardment that was too short and too light. In the south, by Vimy Ridge, the French were able to rain thousands of shells down onto German positions for days before their infantry advanced. The British could not do that. They had neither the guns nor the high explosive shells. The British bombardment lasted just 40 minutes. It was not enough. It was never going to be enough.

On the morning of 9 May, the British artillery opened up at 5.00 am. The infantry lifted out of their trenches at 5.40 am. It was cut down. German machine gunners sat at intervals of 20 yards or so behind broad, deep breastworks. Not only did the bombardment fail to trouble the machine gunners, it also failed to cut the wire in front of the German trenches. The first wave of British infantry slowed after only a few yards. And then halted in front of the German machine guns. Behind them, chaos and congestion. Each wave ran into the one in front. The men were static, easy targets. Of the 11,000 killed or wounded, most fell within a few paces of their trench. No ground was won.

The lessons were clear enough. They underlined what First Ypres had shown. In this new form of warfare, infantry could not hope to make any ground at all unless they attacked after a "long methodical bombardment" that destroyed - not simply damaged or inconvenienced - defences that were strong, well-placed and well-supplied. That bombardment had to be far in excess of anything achieved before. It had to be lengthy, heavy, without a pause for days and nights to destroy the machine guns and "shatter the nerves" of those that survived.

The problem was, the BEF had neither the guns nor the shells to do it. Nor did they in the autumn, at Loos. Haig estimated he'd have neither the men nor the munitions to launch the kind of infantry assault that would have any chance of lasting success until spring 1916. It was a realistic assessment derived from a lesson learned.

But once again, it was a lesson that took second place to the politics of alliance.

***

The futile slaughter at Aubers Ridge had wider repercussions. Back in London, Asquith's Liberal government was in trouble. The news from another front, Gallipoli on the Dardanelles in modern day Turkey, was bad and got worse each day. That operation had stretched British military resources beyond breaking point. In the Dardanelles, men were literally running out of bullets. At one point, the ration was two per man per day. The big guns had next to no shells. It was not that bad on the Western Front but the government's opponents blamed the bloody debacle at Aubers Ridge, in part, to the 'distraction' in the Dardanelles and the shortage of shells it caused.

There was a political price to pay. Winston Churchill, the First Lord of the Admiralty, was the politician more than any other behind the Gallipoli campaign. Its failures were his failures. Pressure on him grew as the prospect of success shrank. The War Secretary, Lord Kitchener, was under pressure, too. He was hugely popular in the country. Less so at Westminster. His opponents claimed he'd failed to make sure the factories had turned out enough shells and guns.

He had enemies outside Westminster, too. They included the Commander in Chief of the British Expeditionary Force, Sir John French. His enmity was personal. He knew the War Secretary thought he was out of his depth - an estimation that was fully justified. But in spite of his own responsibility for the slaughter at Aubers Ridge, Sir John saw in its aftermath the chance to strike at Kitchener. Actively manufacturing a media and political crisis that goes by the name of the 'shells scandal' or 'shells crisis'.

The bare facts are these. Five days after Aubers Ridge, on May 14, the *Times* printed a despatch from its war correspondent at the front, Charles à Court Repington, blaming the disaster on the lack of high explosive shells.

His anonymous account was factually accurate, though fell short of telling the whole story. It ran under the headline: "Need for shells: British attacks checked: Limited supply the cause: A Lesson From France" and went on:

> *"We had not sufficient high explosives to lower the enemy's parapets to the ground ... The want of an unlimited supply of high explosives was a fatal bar to our success"*

There was little that Haig or his generals would have disagreed with in Repington's despatch. But they would have added much and pointed out that the shortage of high-explosive shells was only one factor.

Repington's despatch was designed to damage Lord Kitchener. To blame him singly, directly and personally for the mismanagement that had caused over 10,000 British casualties.

A week later, on 21 May and while British, Dominion and Empire troops were in action at Festubert, the *Daily Mail* recycled the story with no new facts and for no reason other than to underline Kitchener's culpability and to do it so thickly no reader could miss it - an approach to journalism that remains unchanged at the *Mail* to this day. "The

Shells Scandal: Lord Kitchener's Tragic Blunder" was the headline.

The pressure to get a grip on munitions - or, more accurately, give the appearance of getting a grip - became irresistible. Those out for Kitchener's and Churchill's blood could now sniff it.

Asquith met opposition leaders, asked all his ministers to resign and, on May 25, formed a national government containing opposition Conservative and Unionist ministers. They demanded he sack Churchill. He did. They demanded a new post. Minister of Munitions. They got it. And as if to rub salt into Kitchener's wounds, Asquith gave to the job to arch schemer and Kitchener's arch critic, Lloyd George.

But those bare facts tell only part of the story. Currents of political intrigue churned under the surface. Men better suited to settling scores and political infighting failed utterly to show a scrap of leadership when war was wasting the lives of thousands of young British men.

Turning Britain's factories from peace to war was never going to be smooth. And as the nature of the war changed and the demand for high explosive shells soared, there was little chance that demand could be met. At the time of Aubers Ridge, British factories were producing something like 22,000 shells per day – a tenth the number German plants were turning out. Add new fronts like that in the Dardanelles and the shortage became acute. There was a real world crisis. But it is difficult if not impossible to see the 'shells scandal' as an affair whose main purpose was to increase the flow of explosives to British guns.

Its main purpose was to unseat Kitchener. And his political and media enemies were exceptionally powerful. Chief among them, the press baron Lord Northcliffe who, as Alfred Harmsworth, had developed the idea of a British tabloid press and in 1915 owned both the *Times* and the *Daily Mail*.

Northcliffe's loathing owed much to Kitchener's ban on journalists traveling to the front. Northcliffe had tried to get the ban lifted. He went to see Kitchener in the War Office but their meeting ended in a row and Kitchener had Northcliffe thrown out. Their mutual distaste soured further on the day Repington's despatch ran in the *Times*. On that day Northcliffe heard that his favourite nephew, Luke

King, had been killed in action. 'Kitchener murdered him', he was heard to say. That second, direct attack on Kitchener in the *Daily Mail* soon followed.

It was obvious to Kitchener that Northcliffe's papers were prime movers in a plot to oust him from the War Office and slide Lloyd George into his place. Lloyd George himself had already accused Kitchener of lying about the manufacture of high explosive shells.

Whatever the journalistic merit of Repington's reporting, it took second place to the part he played in the political intrigue. Repington was only able to be at the front, let alone report from it, with the connivance of Sir John French, the BEF's C-in-C, whose strategic and tactical clarity in fighting political battles was a marked contrast with his confusion and indecision over real military affairs.

Sir John had already shown his opportunism over the munitions problems in the spring, a couple of months before the 'shells scandal', with an interview in Northcliffe's *Times*. He may indeed have been anxious to increase the flow of arms to the Western Front by going public in that interview. But he was at least as anxious to damage Kitchener. His decision in May to defy Kitchener's ban on journalists and facilitate Repington's trip to the front was just as opportunistic.

It is possible to read Repington's 14 May *Times* despatch, published anonymously, as nothing other than the sober reportage of a seasoned correspondent and former military man. His credentials as a journalist cannot be questioned. Nor his knowledge of military matters. He'd risen to the rank of Lieutenant Colonel in the early 1900s. But his discreditable behaviour in a messy divorce scandal cut short his army career. He had once been a supporter of Kitchener but now found himself among his foes. The reason, he insisted, was that he was moved by the severe losses at Aubers Ridge of his old regiment, the Rifle Brigade. But the fact was, he was only in a position to witness the disaster because Sir John French had defied Kitchener to give him access. He'd only been able to file his despatch with Sir John's help, too. And the information in his despatch that most damaged Kitchener came from a private conversation with Sir John and sight of confidential documents.

It was Sir John, too, who ensured Repington's report, though heavily censored, was published. And he sent aides to London to brief Kitchener's political enemies including Lloyd George, Bonar Law and Balfour, showing them the same documents Repington had seen. It was considerably more decisive, better planned and more effective than anything Sir John achieved on the battlefield.

In the new, coalition cabinet, Kitchener was stripped of responsibility for munitions though not of his seat at the top table and his role in shaping Britain's war. Asquith understood he was too popular to be sacked – an understanding Northcliffe had failed to grasp. After his attack on Kitchener in the *Daily Mail*, the paper's circulation fell 200,000, it was banned from London clubs and burned on the floor of the Stock Exchange. Northcliffe insisted "I mean to tell people the truth and I don't care what it costs".

Among those who found it difficult to excuse Lord Northcliffe and Sir John was the King. In the last week of May, his Assistant Private Secretary and Equerry, Clive Wigram, sent Haig a letter that could not have been written without the King's endorsement. The 'shells scandal' had been, he wrote:

> *"An organised conspiracy in the Press controlled by Lord Northcliffe against Lord Kitchener ... Sir J French's personal staff are mixed up in it ... (who had) approached the editors of the daily Press and asked them to write up Sir J. and blackguard Kitchener!"*

Wigram urged Haig to "have a word with Sir John" to "keep him from quarreling with Kitchener". But Haig records in his diary that his words have "no effect. The truth is that Sir J. is of a very jealous disposition"

***

It is very doubtful that the men on the Western Front knew or cared much about the political scandal in London, though they would certainly have known and felt strongly about the reality that lay behind it; the shortage of munitions. It did, however, enrage the Expeditionary Force's senior officers. General Henry Rawlinson wrote that:

> *"the attack on [Kitchener] is perfectly monstrous, and has raised us out here to a pitch of fury. It is a diabolical plot ... the true cause of our failures is that our tactics have been faulty, and that we have misconceived the strength and resisting power of the enemy ... [to] say that the casualties have been due to the want of H.E. shells (high explosive shells) for the 18-pounders is a perversion of the truth. Feeling out here is one of intense disgust at the initiation of a Press attack when all should be working in combination against the enemy."*

The shortage of high explosive shells continued to occupy Haig's thinking and became a critical factor in his planning in the autumn, though not with the outcome that he might have predicted at the end of May 1915. And it was not just the shortage of shells. There were problems with the big guns, too. On 23 May, Haig reflected in his diary that the shells he *was* able to get his hands on were often faulty and caused the guns to burst. Plus, the shortage of guns meant they were over-worked and the:

> *"... excessive rate of fire by which guns get very so very hot (meant) that High Explosive exploded in the gun!"*

***

On 19 May, a week after Jim and his battalion had arrived in France and while they were billeted at Outtersteene, their senior officers attended a conference in Armentières, a dozen miles to the south-east. There, attached to the Royal Welch Fusiliers, they made a short visit to the trenches south east of the town. They were reconnoitring the battalion's first familiarisation visit to the front line.

Armentières had been a main centre in the British line since it had been retaken in October 1914. It was four or five miles from the front line trenches but remained in the German gunners' sights. Over the course of the war, it was heavily bombarded and few if any buildings were undamaged. Thousands of British soldiers passed through daily. It was a depot for support and communications. The site of Divisional HQs for the sectors of the line on either side. And it hosted a mass of heavy guns. Even so, many French locals

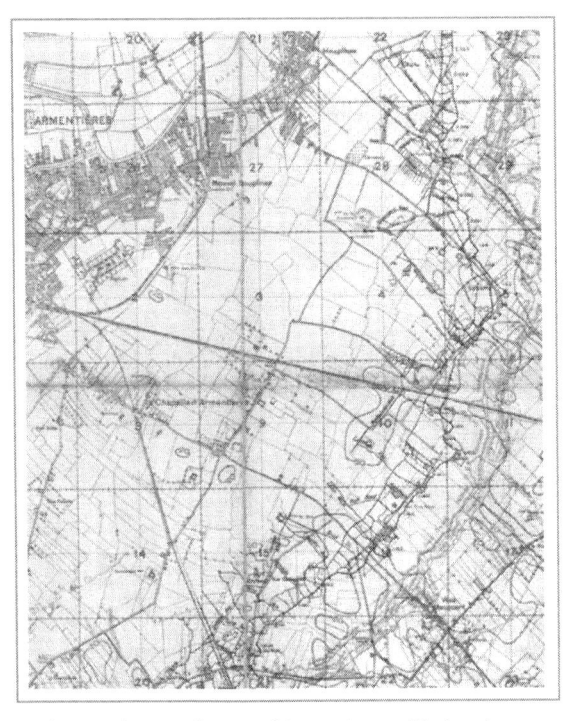

The trenches south east of Armentieres. (National Library of Scotland)

stayed put and while they struggled to find an unbroken roof to sleep under, they ran a multitude of businesses catering to British tastes.

After their first visit to the trenches on the afternoon of the 19th the battalion's officers returned

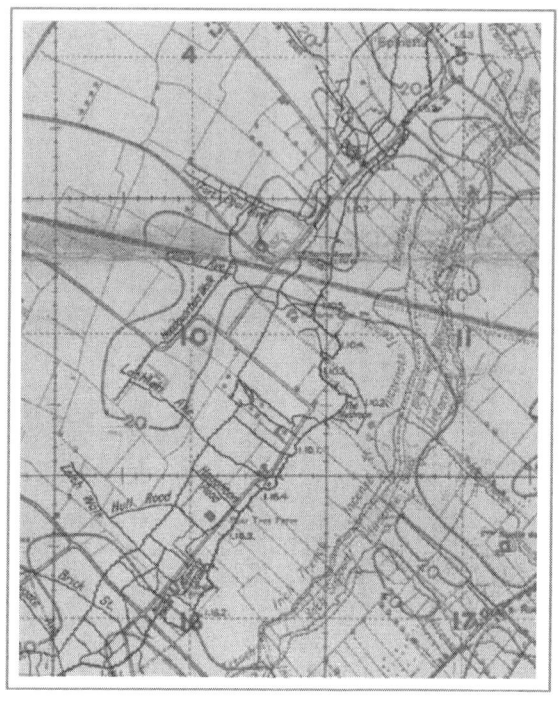

The section of trenches occupied by the 6th King's Own Scottish Borderers in May 1915. (National Library of Scotland)

to Armentières on the afternoon of the 20th. The following day, 21 May, they continued with their familiarisation and briefings in Armentières, conferring with their officer counterparts in the Fusiliers.

On Saturday 22 May, the battalion left Outtersteene and marched the ten miles or so to Armentières where they arrived at 2 pm. They spent the afternoon in final preparations for their brief stay at the front and at 8 pm made the short march to the trenches. The four companies of the battalion were each attached to units in the sector of trenches to the south and south-east of Armentières. From the Rue du Bois in the south – now an industrial estate close to the A25 motorway – to L'Epinette in the north – then and now a tiny hamlet. In some places, the British and German front line trenches were no more than 90 yards apart.

The section of trench they occupied this time was almost due east of Chapelle d'Armentieres, to the south of the main railway line to Lille.

In the centre of the section, sap trenches snaked outwards to a forward line creating a quadrangle called 'The Mushroom'. At the same point, the German line bulged too. Here, no man's land was no more than fifty or sixty yards wide. Patrols were frequent and dangerous.

Getting to and from the front line here was not easy. To the south of the section was a communication trench called Lothian Road. That was a longer trench and tended to be kept in good condition. But it was a long way round to reach the fire trenches. A more direct communication trench, Argyle Road was often heavily shelled and was used only at night. Pioneer Road was new and still being completed when Jim's battalion was in the sector. While at the north end, men had to use a communication trench belonging to the adjoining brigade to get to their fire trench.

The bulges in the line – the salients – meant that the two companies who occupied them were exposed to field gun fire, mortars and sniping from their flanks. The trenches themselves were narrow and deep but, according to one senior officer, the dugouts were "bad and dangerous". The support line here was incomplete with practically no dugouts.

They were not the first battalion of the 'new armies' to familiarise themselves in this part of the line that summer. It was a relatively stable sector and relatively quiet – though the use of the word 'quiet' or 'normal' in battalion diaries is telling. One entry reads: "Normal day. Sgt Kelly is killed". And a 'quiet day' might be a day on which there was sniping only in the morning or afternoon and only one or two mortars that crashed into trenches repaired the day before.

Because of that relative stability, a semi-permanent ecology had developed behind static front lines. From above, the area looked more like a city than a military deployment. Being so close to Armentières, it was the obvious place to give the 'new armies' their first taste of action. The day before the Borderers made their visit, the 11th Royal Scots were there. And the day after they withdrew, the 8th Black Watch followed them in.

The hosts for these brief visits were battalions of the regular army who had been in France since autumn 1914, though few men who'd crossed the Channel in that first BEF deployment were still alive or still in the trenches. The reserves and territorials who'd replaced them, though, were battle hardened and by now had spent months doing their turns of duty.

That first acclimatisation visit was not without peril. While Jim and his battalion were returning to billets in Armentières at 10 pm on 23 May, two enemy shells caught 2 Platoon, 'A' company wounding 2 NCOs and 3 men. A Lance Corporal was later found to be missing.

After a night in Armentières, Jim's battalion returned to billets in and near Outtersteene where they stayed until June 5. The highpoint of their time there was doubtless a visit by Sir John French, at noon on 29 May.

Billets

Battalion war diaries vary enormously in the stories they tell and the detail they give. Especially when a battalion was away from the lines, in billets. Some give a vivid picture of daily life. Training and drill. Marches, visits and church parades. Fetching and carrying. Fatigue parties. Indiscipline, courts martial and field punishments. Others do not. Lieutenant Colonel A.D.G. Maclean, the 6th battalion's commanding officer, was one who committed the bare minimum to paper. Laconic even by Spartan standards. Days, weeks are dismissed with 'battalion remained in billets' or just 'in billets'.

Lt Colonel Maclean's terseness hides much. We know nearly nothing of his battalion's daily life in billets and not much more of how it lived in the trenches. We have to infer what we can from the more eloquent diaries of new army battalions who stayed in similar billets and were at a similar stage of training and readiness. The 8th Gordon Highlanders, for example, or the 11th Highland Light Infantry - battalions the Borderers fought alongside in the summer of 1915.

'Billets' could mean anything. For some, usually officers, it would mean a room in a French family's home. For others, a corner of a field with only a greatcoat for groundsheet and blanket. Somewhere between the two were damaged and abandoned buildings. Houses, schools, shops, stables. The large barns that littered the countryside were popular with billeting officers, less so with the men. And there were tents or bivouacs.

Feeding and fetching for the thousands of British soldiers billeted in Flanders and Artois kept many French businesses going. Estaminets changed their menus to include egg and chips to meet British tastes. Householders turned rooms into small shops selling beer, cigarettes, chocolate and postcards. Children ran the lanes and alleyways selling fruit and sweets - though the cute photographs and drawings that appeared in British newspapers and magazines skated over the reality that such children were often abandoned, orphans or a French family's only breadwinner. And brothels were everywhere, though many hardly deserved the name.

Daily life in billets was filled with drill, training, more drill, marching and more drill. There was training in the skills of trench warfare. The Borderers spent hours perfecting bomb throwing – an expertise that never quite made up for the inferiority of the British grenades. Machine gunners and snipers trained and practiced. And all, day in, day out, bashed through infantry skills. Shooting, bayonet work, charging. Long marches with full kit along roads that were by turns ankle deep in water and dry, dusty white chalk. There was PT, parades and square bashing.

Hours that were not given over to drill and training were filled with hard, physical work. Things were fetched. Things were carried. Working parties would dig trenches, mend roads, clear ditches, bury the dead. Even collect the harvest.

If we had only Colonel Maclean's word for it, the 6th Borderers were paragons of military discipline. There is not a single record of a man being court martialled or punished for drunkenness, absence without leave, insubordination, foul language to officers or any one of the many offences a soldier might commit. It is unlikely his was the only battalion in the British army manned with those who never erred.

We know from other war diaries that officers would hold frequent courts martial. Often dealing with a job lot of offenders. We know how common FP1 - or 'Field Punishment No.1' - was. Indeed, in the course of the war, it was used on over 60,000 recorded occasions. It had been introduced in the 1880s to replace flogging and entailed the man being tied or fettered to some immovable object - a fence post or a gun wheel, say - for up to two hours a day, three days out of four for up to 21 days. And he'd lose pay. Or, if he was an NCO, lose a rank or more. Some saw a spell of No.1 as a badge of honour, especially if it was to punish a man who'd given an unpopular NCO a hard time.

The were letters and parcels from home. Tens of thousands of them. Some men got a parcel every other day. The BEF's postal service was in itself a marvel of organisation.

We do not know how many letters or postcards Jim got or sent. Three of those he sent survive. They are brief and lack any description of life - but that would almost certainly have been cut by the censors anyway. We learn nothing of the detail of his four moves from billet to billet in June 1915 while plans for the Battle of Loos took shape.

***

The month began with a heatwave, the battalion strength 29 officers and 950 men. It was inevitable after the late spring failures that the French high command would turn again to a 'big push' on that German line that bulged so offensively into Artois and Champagne. While the British were still regrouping after the battle of Festubert, Marshall Foch was pressing the BEF's C-in-C, Sir John French, to begin planning for just such a new joint offensive.

These were early days. And while at the end of May and beginning of June, Foch seemed indifferent to the precise point the British should mount their offensive, he did propose they extend their line south of the La Bassée canal at Givenchy towards Loos. By doing that, Foch argued, they could cover the left of the French Tenth Army as it tried once again to retake Vimy Ridge.

Haig was reluctant. If the British were to attack in another 'big push', it should be somewhere on the existing line. He sensed, though, that his C-in-C, Sir John French had, as usual, adopted as his own the last idea he'd heard. Sir John, Haig thought, "hankers after Loos" following his conversation with Foch. If that were so, it was not for very long. Sir John's constant changes of mind were a defining feature of the planning for the Battle of Loos.

Haig met Sir John to discuss options on Monday 31 May. There were only two, he thought, and one was much better than the other. That was to carry on with operations "as now", in the Aubers/Festubert area, and combine that with an attack south of the canal "if ammunition suffices for both". Haig knew it would not. The other was to "stop present operations entirely, and transfer bag and baggage to opposite Loos" which, Haig thought, would mean:

> *"throwing away such advantages as we have already gained, and then if the French do not succeed in gaining Vimy plateau, we shall be unable to do anything at all."*

Sir John seemed persuaded. But not for long. A few days later, on 4 June, Foch revealed his latest thinking. Central to that was a major British infantry attack south of the canal, on the German trenches north of Loos.

It was thinking that would dominate Franco-British politics and military planning for the next four months.

***

Jim's battalion had come to the end of its billet in or near Outtersteene. On 5 June, the heatwave returned after 24 hours of summer rain and that evening, at 8 pm, the men paraded and marched fifteen miles or so south west to Bourecq, a scattering of small brick houses around a Mairie and a church. In most ways indistinguishable from Outtersteene, though further back from the front.

And rather than a crossroads at its centre, like Outtersteene, Bourecq had and has a 'T' junction.

The battalion stayed there for a little over a week until, at 10.30 pm on 14 June after a fine warm day, they marched via Lillers to new billets in and around Robecq.

That march to Robecq took the Borderers closer to the front line. Just ten miles west of Aubers. They did not know it, but they came very close - within an hour - to being thrown into one of the minor battles of that summer. What became known as the Second Action at Givenchy.

Joffre had persisted in pressing Sir John to extend the British line south of the La Bassée canal. At the end of May, Sir John agreed to a five mile extension taking over French trenches from Festubert to Cuinchy, just south of the canal. A few days later, again at French insistence, he agreed to extend the line northwards too to occupy the whole of the Ypres salient.

These extensions to the British line had an important consequence for the arrival of the 'new armies'. The original intention was to have those three divisions of keen, fresh volunteers strengthen the existing line. Lift some of the pressure from the regulars and territorials who'd held fast for over nine months. Instead, they enabled a broader front.

Taking over the new section of the line was not easy. Exhausted troops who had fought at Aubers Ridge - those that had survived the slaughter - were ordered south into the new section. There, they found that German snipers were hyperactive. Volley after volley of trench mortars arced into their new trenches. German miners had dug a warren of tunnels under them and were able to explode one mine after another.

In early June, Sir John French gave the order, effectively, to go easy. The only offensive operations should be "small aggressive threats which will not require much ammunition or many troops". There was little other option in reality; for all the political ructions in Westminster over the 'shells scandal', heavy ammunition was still in short supply; and the 'new armies' were only now being rotated into the trenches.

Joffre had a different idea. He wanted to keep up the pressure in Artois. With an attack during June by French troops from trenches north of Loos that the British would occupy in the autumn. He demanded a

British flanking attack in support. An assault on a low rise that the Germans occupied at Violaines, north east of La Bassée. A lip of land that looked over the ground north of Loos from a height little more than that of a man on stilts.

This did not quite fit Sir John's description of a "small aggressive threat". But the French had asked and the French would get. The action was planned for 2 June. Then postponed to 11 June. Then postponed again. The French were not ready. Finally, the infantry attacked on the night of the 15/16 June.

The British artillery opened up 48 hours before. On the night of the 13 June. The aim, once again, was to silence the German machine gunners and cut the wire in no-man's land. But, once again, the 'slow' bombardment failed. It had to be 'slow' to eke out the limited munitions they had.

The attack, when it came, was a complete failure. Utterly pointless.

Just before 6pm, British tunnelers exploded a mine under the German trenches. Moments later, the infantry went over. Moments later, machine gunners cut them down. Moments later the men counted the cost. In two infantry companies, 360 officers and men were reduced to 72. In moments.

Huge losses for no gain did not deter the generals in Divisional HQ. They ordered another attack. In moments they were forced to understand that the shattered men in shattered units could not make that second attack. Dead men cannot charge. They called it off. But only until relief battalions could move up.

It was chaos.

Stretcher bearers trying to get to the rear with the dead and wounded crashed into units trying to go forwards. Orders got lost in the confusion. It took forever to get the relieving units up to the line.

That second attack was supposed to go in at 1.30 am. Then at 5.30 am. Finally, it began at 4.45 on the afternoon of 16 June. And it was another catastrophic slaughter. The men of one battalion saw half its men hit before they'd even got through their own wire. Others fell as they waited to go over. A handful made it across almost to the German trenches and survived to make it back to the British lines. They crawled back during the night of the 16/17 June and reported that the German riflemen firing on them had been standing in ranks, two or three deep in their trench with another line behind them handing out ammunition to ensure the rifles never stopped firing.

Over 1,000 officers and men were lost. Many of them had just returned to the front line after recovering from wounds sustained at the Battle of Ypres. One brigade had been involved in major attacks three times in four months.

Jim and his battalion narrowly escaped playing a part in this Second Action at Givenchy. In their billets in and around Robecq, orders came at 11.30 am on 15 June that they should be ready to move at one hour's notice any time after 6 am the following day. They would have heard the bombardment just over the horizon, a half day's march away. Their orders were for 'destination unknown' but everyone knew that when the order came, it would be to march towards the sound of those guns.

They spent the rest of that day getting their kit, wagons and transport ready to move. There were parades and inspections and as a Lance Corporal, Jim would have been responsible for making sure the men in his section, in his platoon were ready to go the following morning.

The men stood-to just before dawn on 16 June. Their weapons and kit inspected. From 6 am it was a question of waiting. Waiting for the order to move. Fully kitted. As time passed, there'd have been the usual round of drill and inspections. When night fell, there was no standing down. They had to stay at an hour's notice and stayed so for five days. In the end, they went nowhere. The fighting at Givenchy ended. And with it, the urgency to move up to the line.

On 18 June, they took on 50 new rank and file and for the next ten days remained in billets, 'stood down'. The new men more than replaced the 21 taken off the battalion strength, sick or injured. Reasons unknown.

***

The failed attack at Givenchy was of little consequence in the great scheme of things.

While the 6th Borderers were in Bourecq and Robecq, French and British generals were working on plans for what became the Battle of Loos. History has been harsh on them. Good military sense and lessons learned from Ypres, Aubers and Festubert were passed over to accommodate the demands of alliance. Those conflicting French and British perspectives over the relative merits of attack and defence stayed unresolved. French suspicions of

British commitment and motives grew. The origin of the phrase 'lions led by donkeys' is obscure - by some accounts, it dates from the Crimean War - but what is certain is its perfect application to the planning and conduct of the Battle of Loos.

Foch's plan, presented at that 4 June conference, bristled with optimism and bravado. Both were calculated to counter what he and Joffre saw as defeatism in the French political establishment whom they constantly suspected of looking for any chance to make peace with Germany. Both were unjustified by the facts on the ground yet they were the flywheel that kept up the momentum towards Loos. It was a momentum that, perversely, was also in part sustained by French suspicion of British intent and the British C-in-C, Sir John French's indecisiveness. An indecisiveness that derived from his feeble grasp on affairs and from his knowledge that French suspicions of his true intentions were fully justified.

Foch's broad plan was not dissimilar from the one that had failed in the spring and early summer. Except it was grander. Again, it called for two crushing blows to the German occupiers, though this time in two widely separated sectors of the Western Front, in Artois and in Champagne. Again, the plan was to force the Germans to retreat, at the very least from French soil if not all the way back to Berlin. The first step on the road to total victory:

> *"A successful break-through both in Champagne and in Artois was to be followed immediately by a general offensive of all the French and British armies on the Western Front which will compel the Germans to retreat beyond the Meuse and possibly end the war ..."*

... Joffre wrote to Sir John French.

It overlooked many military realities and ignored what was becoming more clear as each day passed. That the German lines were too strong, too well manned, too well supplied and too well armed to be swept aside by anything the Allies had been able to muster so far.

Sir John's first instinct, unsurprisingly, was to agree, broadly, with Joffre's plan. An agreement that derived as much from his belief that Joffre was an ally in his loathing for Kitchener as anything else. It certainly did not derive from any hard headed military assessment of what was, by any measure, a flawed plan.

Joffre was by now pushing hard for the British to stretch their line yet further south and onto new ground facing the mining towns of Auchy les Mines, Haines and Hulluch. Given the scale of the demand, Sir John decided it might be a good idea to take a look at the ground between the La Bassée canal and Loos for himself. In the second week of June, he went with Foch to the trenches there, held at the time by the French, and found that:

> "*the ground ... affords many advantages to an attacker ...*"

It is difficult to understand what Sir John meant. It was military nonsense. The only possible explanation is that he was parroting his French host's bravado and optimism.

Whatever the explanation, he asked Haig to begin making detailed plans. Haig recorded the order in his diary:

> "*to view the situation and if necessary extend my right (i.e. to the south of the La Bassée Canal) with the object of getting*

> *ground suitable for the attack against Loos".*

The following Sunday afternoon, June 20, Haig drove down to Saines-en-Gohelle and then rode on horseback up to the low heights of the Bois de Bouvigny from where he could look out over the ground around Loos. He was not encouraged:

> *"the country is covered with coal pits and houses. The towns of Lievin, Lens etc run into one another. This all renders the problem of an attack in this area very difficult"*

Haig's assessment might have been influenced by his clear preference to stay on the ground he knew, strengthen his positions there and mount an attack when men and munitions allowed.

But he was not alone in seeing the drawbacks in the ground around Loos. Drawbacks Sir John had failed to notice. Generals Horne and Haking also looked for themselves. They were not encouraged, either:

> *"The Enemy has greatly strengthened his position. A second line with wire*

> *entanglement is distinctly visible here ... it would be possible to capture the Enemy's first line of trenches (say a length of 1200 yards) opposite Maroc (i.e. west of Loos) but it would not be possible to advance beyond, because our own artillery could not support us, as ground immediately in our front cannot be seen from any part of our front. On the other hand the Enemy has excellent observing stations for his artillery."*

And one of Haig's corps commanders, Sir Henry Rawlinson who, in due course, was entrusted with detailed planning for the battle was equally damning:

> *"My new front is as flat as the palm of my hand. Hardly any cover anywhere ... it will cost us dearly and we will not get very far."*

It is difficult to imagine a more negative assessment.

Haig's final thought was to recall the lessons of Ypres, Aubers and Festubert:

> *"The Enemy's defences are now so strong that they can only be taken by siege methods – by using bombs, and by hand to hand fighting in the trenches – the ground above is so swept by gun and machine gun and rifle fire that an advance in the open, except by night, is impossible."*

Sir John changed his mind. After he'd heard and seen Haig's judgments, he decided that Joffre's plans were "causing me a good deal of anxious thought":

> *"after careful examination of the ground at Loos and Lens and a consideration of Haig's report I am doubtful of the success of an attack against these places, which I had arranged with the French to make."*

Joffre was dismissive. He swept all objections aside - the pattern for the next three months:

> *"your attack will find particularly favourable ground between Loos and La Bassée"*

Sir John changed his mind.

Haig's reservations about the proposed battlefield were sharpened by another serious problem that had still not been overcome. The shortage of heavy guns and high explosive shells. He would need huge numbers of both for any attack to stand the slightest chance. While manufacture and supply were picking up, neither was yet close to what was needed. Nor would it be, according to the best estimates, until early 1916.

There was, however, an alternative. Gas. While banned by international conventions, it had already been used on the Western Front and its military effects found in some respects to be potentially greater than artillery.

Two international conventions drawn up at the Hague in 1899 and 1907 banned the use of gas and chemical agents in warfare. In spite of that, the French had used tear gas - 'lachrymosing agents' - in 1914. More lethally, the Germans had used chlorine gas. The first time, at Bolimov on the Eastern Front, it was a failure. It was so cold the gas froze. The second time, in the Second Battle of Ypres in April 1915. It was devastating.

In that battle, German engineers released 168 tons of gas against French Algerian troops. The wind was ideal and within a few moments the gas cloud covered some 10,000 men. Half were dead within ten minutes. The remainder were blinded. At best temporarily, at worst permanently. Of those who survived, 2,000 coughing, stumbling men were taken prisoner. The Germans used chlorine a second time at Ypres, against Canadian troops. But this time they lacked the element of surprise. The Canadians were prepared and protected and the attacking German infantry suffered heavily. From then, in the sporadic fighting around Ypres, the Germans made repeated use of gas.

Publicly, the British C-in-C Sir John French was outraged. It was a … :

> "… *cynical and barbarous disregard of the well-known usages of civilised war and a flagrant defiance of the Hague Convention."*

The notion that the war in France and Flanders conformed to any notion of 'civilised' jars now. But Sir John maintained the public outrage in his despatch of 15 June, printed in the London Gazette of 10 July:

> *"All the scientific resources of Germany have apparently been brought into play to produce a gas of so virulent and poisonous a nature that any human being brought into contact with it is first paralysed and then meets with a lingering and agonising death. The enemy has invariably preceded, prepared and supported his attacks by a discharge in stupendous volume of these poisonous gas fumes whenever the wind was favourable ... The brain power and thought which has evidently been at work before this unworthy method of making war reached the pitch of efficiency which has been demonstrated in its practice shows that the Germans must have harboured these designs for a long time. As a soldier I cannot help expressing the deepest regret and some surprise that an Army which hitherto has claimed to be the chief exponent of the chivalry of war should have stooped to employ such devices against brave and gallant foes."*

Guarbecque Church

By the time this despatch was published, however, the BEF generals were already discussing how they too could use chlorine. On Wednesday July 7, the Director of Gas Services for the BEF, Lt Colonel Foulkes, met Haig to work out how to use it on the battlefield at Loos.

***

In the Artois countryside, Jim's battalion was changing billets once again.

On June 28 at 4.45 pm, the men paraded in the rain and marched five miles west, along the Canal d'Aire, to Guarbecque, another typical northern French village, where they spent two days in billets in mostly wet, damp and rainy weather with the occasional bright spell.

Once again, they were under orders to be ready to move quickly and to an unknown destination.

Plans

The high summer of 1915 in northern France was one of alternating heat waves and torrential rain with cold easterly winds. It was weather that matched the indecision and changes of plan in Allied military minds.

During June and July, British and French generals met in four major conferences, each in an atmosphere of suspicion and evasion. The French suspected the British had no intention of actually fighting in the planned autumn offensive. It was a justified suspicion. Sir John French was attracted to the idea of cooperating with the French attack:

"... by threat and implication".

That meant giving the Germans every reason to believe an infantry attack from British lines was imminent ... without one actually being launched. Instead, he imagined:

> *"a storm of artillery fire laid down for a period of days ... (to) harass and destroy (German) forward elements and lead them to believe that a heavy attack might follow at any moment".*

There were two major flaws in his thinking. First, laying down a storm of artillery fire needed high explosive shells in quantities his divisions did not have, in spite of Lloyd George's appointment as Munitions Minister. Second, there was no question of telling the French. And Sir John's evasions over this fundamental question angered Joffre. He had little faith in British intentions right up to the day of the battle. And that lack of faith caused him to ensure the most extreme political pressure was applied to Sir John, something the British C-in-C he was temperamentally ill-equipped to resist.

And so, for example, at the Frevent conference on 27 July, Foch brushed aside what he both knew and imagined were British objections to the French plan. It was, he insisted:

> *"of vital importance, regardless of the ground and strength of the enemy's defences, the British First Army should make its attack south of the canal in co-operation with the French".*

Foch's and Joffre's determination to ensure that happened never wavered. And their suspicions over Sir John's intentions were confirmed when, in an extraordinary act of betrayal, his Chief of Staff, Field Marshall Sir William Robertson, told his French opposite number exactly what Sir John was contemplating.

When Joffre learned, he saw it as insubordination. He banged a metaphorical fist on British War Secretary Lord Kitchener's, desk, warning that if the British were to slink away from what he saw as their duty, his own days as 'generalissimo' were numbered and the defeatists in the French political class would sue for peace with Germany. He also wrote a note to Sir John, intended as something of a spanking. Sir John's reply was evasive. He would, he said, 'assist according to ammunition'. A meaningless answer from a man who thought pounding German trenches with TNT he did not have and had no prospect of getting was an alternative to an infantry attack.

For Haig and his senior officers, the high summer of 1915 was enormously frustrating. He continued to argue that if there were to be a major infantry attack, it should be to the north and not the south of the La Bassée canal. For a brief moment, he thought Sir John had accepted his reasoning. Except that he - Sir John - wrote at the same time to Joffre telling him the British would do whatever Joffre 'thinks best'. When Haig learnt about this he despaired. Sir John had, he wrote:

> *"(put) himself and the British Forces unreservedly in Joffre's hands".*

The BEF's C-in-C was now proving dangerously unpredictable. At a conference in St Omer on Saturday 7 August, Sir John told Haig bluntly that he had agreed to Joffre's plan and the British First Army would attack German positions south of the canal. Yet he insisted at the same time that he disagreed with it. He was still holding onto the notion that 'attack' did not necessarily mean an infantry attack. Haig's understanding of Sir John's muddled thinking was that:

> *"my attack is to be made chiefly with artillery and I am not to launch a large force of infantry to the attack of objectives which are so strongly held as to be liable to result only in the sacrifice of many lives".*

Sir John's reluctance to commit to a massive land battle did not rule out other, frankly insane, ideas. Including one for a sacrificial diversion - an attack on one of the strongest forts anywhere on the German line. The Hohenzollern Redoubt. A steel and concrete lined fortress dug into a low slagheap near Auchy les Mines just south of the La Bassée canal. He even dreamed that such an attack might not end in disaster and that it might be followed by an advance on Hulluch.

It was more than insane. By any modern test it was immoral. It shrugged away the sacrifice of thousands of British lives to distract the attention of a few thousand German troops from a French advance. But it remained an option right up to the morning of the battle.

The option of an infantry attack along a broad front supported by gas was, however, beginning to take hold on British military minds. With hindsight, it is difficult to understand why.

Set aside the international conventions and the moral repugnance that underlay those conventions. Set aside that everyone now knew what it did to men's lungs and eyes and skin, inflicting a living death on those who survived its use. Set all of that aside and the fact remained that gas was a weapon that made little military sense in support of a mass infantry advance.

It maimed and killed men and corroded their weapons - but it was unreliable. It could be neither ranged nor aimed. All was down to the strength and direction of the wind. Plus, its effects, as the Germans found at Ypres, relied on surprise. Even rudimentary gas masks lessened its lethal effect.

But there was something even more important. Even if all else was right, gas could not cut barbed wire or scramble booby traps. It did not wreck enemy trenches or shift the obstacles that held up the infantry and turned men into targets.

For all that, Haig and his subordinates put steadily more and more faith in chlorine gas. Not just to support a small scale attack on the Hohenzollern Redoubt but to be the prelude to the massive assault Joffre was demanding - a demand Joffre still believed the British would not fulfil. On Thursday 12 August, he wrote to Sir John that British support for the French offensive:

> *"can only be effective if it takes the form of a large and powerful attack, composed of the maximum force you have available, executed with the hope of success and carried through to the end".*

While Sir John nodded his assent, he still kept in his own head the option of 'defensive support'. And Joffre's suspicion deepened.

By now though, six weeks from the eventual date of the battle, it was becoming clear that if there was to be the massive attack Joffre demanded, it could only be mounted from British lines with the use of gas.

***

If the British generals, planning over the lunch tables in the chateaux of northern France, were intent on keeping options open, others were not. It was politicians in London who made the critical decisions that eventually pushed six British divisions into battle near Loos. Decisions made under pressure from Paris.

The stalemate on the Western Front was beginning to look permanent by the summer of 1915. But things were different in the east. Anxieties had sharpened over Russia's ability to stay in the war.

News from there had started bad and got worse. Both French and British ministers feared that Russia's exit from the war was only a matter of time. The news from the Dardanelles was no better. That attempt to strike at the Ottomans, Germany's and Austro-Hungary's ally, had become another bloody fiasco. By the 'Black August' of 1915, War Secretary Lord Kitchener was in search of success somewhere. For the good of his reputation as much as the course of the war.

Kitchener's role in ensuring the British took a full and active role in the offensive at Loos was decisive. That much we know for sure. But to this day, we do not know exactly what that role was. There is strong evidence, but no proof, that on 7 July 1915 at an Allied conference in Calais, he struck a secret deal with Joffre to give the French the offensive support they demanded for their Artois/Champagne offensive. And that the deal was unqualified.

Early that morning, before that day's business of the conference proper began, Kitchener and Joffre took a walk together. In private. They continued their private conversation later, on the train that had brought the French contingent north. Once the conference resumed, Joffre appeared publicly to have been brought round to the view that British support in any autumn offensive should be essentially defensive. Lots of sound and fury, but no massed infantry attack.

It was a deception. Joffre left the conference and continued to plan exactly as before, for a major battle in the Loos area with the British fully committed to offence. It is fair to conclude that he believed Sir John French and Haig would fall into line in the end because Kitchener had promised him

- secretly, privately - exactly that. It is just possible that Kitchener hoped he would be able to wriggle out of any secret deal if a renewed offensive in the Dardanelles were successful. If so, he was to be disappointed. By mid-August, Gallipoli was heading for total catastrophe. Kitchener had no option but to deliver on his secret agreement with Joffre.

Haig records in his diary what was clearly an awkward conversation between himself and Kitchener. The conversation that put an end to any idea of 'defensive' support. It happened when Kitchener visited Haig in France on 19 August. He argued passionately that Britain could not stand by and watch their ally, Russia, knocked out. They were on their last legs and it was uncertain how much longer they could go on. It was a crisis and it had made him change his mind. Until now, he told Haig, he'd thought it might be possible to support the French without a massive infantry attack. But not any more. Haig recorded in his diary:

> *"The situation in Russia had caused him to modify these views. He now felt the Allies must act vigorously in order to take some of the pressure off Russia if possible*

> *... we must act with all our energy, and do our utmost to help the French, even though, by doing so, we suffered very heavy losses indeed".*

Winston Churchill, no longer First Lord of the Admiralty but still a member of the government, recorded something similar when Kitchener revealed the same to him. Kitchener was, Churchill wrote, nervous and reticent:

> *"he had an air of suppressed excitement like a man who has taken a great decision of terrible uncertainty, and is about to put it into execution"*

After some hesitation, he finally told Churchill he'd agreed to a "great offensive in France". Churchill replied with no hesitation that there was no chance of success.

***

At the beginning of July, Jim and his battalion were nearing the time when they would finally take their posts in the trenches. They'd narrowly avoided being pushed into the fight around Givenchy in mid-June. Now, though, the time had come for the 'new armies' to begin to take the places of the regulars, reservists and territorials who'd been on the front line for almost a year.

At 4 pm on 30 June, the battalion of 29 officers and 976 men paraded in Guarbecque and marched to new billets near Locon, a small town just a couple of miles behind the line. Like many such towns, it had, by the summer of 1915, become used to British troops on their way to and from the trenches near Festubert. It had suffered considerable damage as a result. At the end of the war, though, the final offensives and counter-offensives left it little more than a pile of rubble and a name on a map.

Trenches

At 5.30 pm on 7 July - the late afternoon of the day on which Kitchener and Joffre made their secret agreement - Jim and his battalion paraded in Locon. They were about to march to their first tour of duty in the front line trenches.

They had been training and preparing for almost a year. Since mid-May, in France, in the Artois countryside around Bourecq, Robecq, Guarbecque and Locon. It had been the repetition of drills and training they'd gone through again and again in Hampshire. Marching, standing-to, saluting, shooting, bayoneting, bomb throwing. More importantly, they were learning how to work as a battalion, as companies, as platoons. Learning how to fight as a unit, follow orders, watch each other's backs.

But as the time had neared, the time they were to enter the war proper, they began to learn the new science of trench warfare. And it was a new science. One whose finding had been done in shrapnel, high explosives, mechanised gunfire, blood and mud. At Ypres, Aubers and Festubert.

They dug practice trenches, learnt how to fire trench mortars and Lewis guns, how to stay safe - or as safe as possible - below the parapet and, of course, how to go over the top. Battalion and company commanders rewrote the manuals on every aspect of war, trying to fit old disciplines to the new world. Officers and men alike were adjusting to the notion that the Western Front stalemate might not be broken for a long time.

Dozens of manuals were written, some with, most without a realistic understanding of trench warfare. The most detailed and most authoritative by far was that written by Major E.B. North of the 124th Infantry Brigade. Major North's *Trench Standing Orders*, though undated, was clearly compiled during late 1915 and written at the end of that year or the beginning of 1916. It is puritanical at times - the Major's recommendations on rum and drunkenness were made more in hope than expectation. Idealistic at others - his advice on the care of men's feet was a counsel of perfection, largely impractical and followed less often that was ideal. But his manual does at least try to spell out in fine detail what was different, new, about the texture of trench warfare. Especially when compared with the corpus of military knowledge learned in colonial wars in India and South Africa.

Trench warfare was an accident. Neither France and her Allies nor Germany and hers went into the war intending it to be the filthy, degrading, semi-subterranean, mutual siege that it became. The opposite. The German war plan called for a rapid advance through Belgium and Artois to Paris. To knock France out of the war within six weeks and allow German military minds to turn east, to Russia alone. The British 'War Book' – the encyclopaedia that set out line by line how to organise for a continental war - required men and equipment to move quickly and called for 120,000 horses to be commandeered to make sure it could happen. For the first few weeks of the war, British and German cavalry charged and chased each other over rolling farmland and through forests in clashes that would have been familiar to a 19th and even 18th century dragoon. One of the first Germans to die in the war did so on the point of a British cavalryman's sabre.

The first holes that the infantrymen dug in Belgium and northern France were the holes that infantrymen had always dug. To defend and protect themselves. Defend and protect their positions. Where they did not or could not dig, they built 'breastworks', humps of earth that formed a kind of trench above the surface.

Even before the First Battle of Ypres in October 1914 - the battle that more than any other defined what was to come - those holes had lengthened to short stretches of trench and began to link one to another. Growing organically into fragile threads of shallow ditches, at first a few hundred yards and then a few miles long. The so-called 'race to the sea' shot both sides' trenches out to the channel ports. But it was not until then, until the First Battle of Ypres and that 'race to the sea', that the generals began to realise this was now the norm. That it was not going to be the war described in the War Book.

That there would be no more cavalry charges. The war on the Western Front went underground. By the end of the year, ever-deeper trenches stretched from the Swiss border to the Channel.

In this strange kind of non-siege siege, each side for the most part watched and waited. Both sides were readily supplied and reinforced. Behind the front lines, communication trenches linked to pre-war networks of roads and railways. Further back, garrisons, command posts, kitchens and field ambulance stations, dugouts and redoubts. Sap trenches stuck out at right angles from the front line into no-man's land to get a gun or a mortar closer to the enemy.

A hundred years on, trenches are the defining image of the war. They are the war. Everything we think we know about the war comes from the image we have of the trenches. But we do not see them as Jim and his battalion saw them.

A hundred years on, we know what trench warfare became. That it was not a temporary, necessary, uncomfortable phase before the war resumed a familiar shape of advances and retreats over open ground. Before riflemen and grenadiers could march in formation to crush the enemy on battlefields Wellington would have recognised and chase the Germans back to Berlin.

A hundred years on, we are shocked by the mud and the rats and the lice and the fear and the randomness of death.

It is inconceivable. Or at least, we can only conceive it with twenty first century minds. Wondering at the futility of it all.

Yet for working-class men like Jim, who'd dashed to join the 'new armies', the trenches were a transitional phase, to endure for a while. Until the real fight began. In the meantime, daily life in the trenches was grim - but no worse than they'd prepared for. And as some old soldiers would say in later life - perhaps with a touch of mischievous overstatement - life in the trenches was not so much worse than that in the mines of Yorkshire and Nottinghamshire. Most of the time it was not much more dangerous, they would half joke - though there is some truth in it. And there were the compensations of comradeship and frequent food.

***

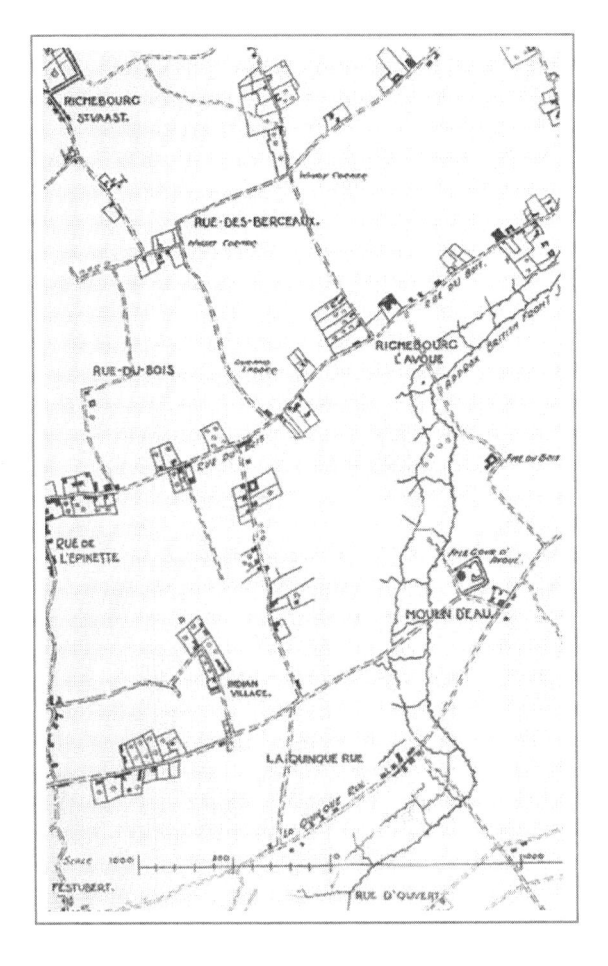

When Jim and his battalion paraded late on the afternoon of 7 July, it was to march to a sector of the trenches between Festubert and Richebourg, east

"These were dank fields"

of Locon. A sector where British and Canadian troops had captured and held German trenches, and with them a few yards of ground, in the May battles.

These were dank fields. Natural streams and man-made dykes cut across them. By mid-1915, a bewildering web of trenches cut even deeper, their floors below the water table, rarely less than ankle deep in water and mud.

The battalion was supposed to take its place in the front line two days earlier, on the night of 5 July. But the handover was delayed. We do not know why. What we do know, however, is that because of the delay, the 6th King's Own Scottish Borderers' first full day in the trenches was not the torrid affair it might have been. On 6 July, the trenches they were due to occupy came under a fierce bombardment that lasted most of the day. In the worst incident, German trench mortars smashed the parapet in three places. One man was buried under the debris. He died. Another was killed by shrapnel. Nine other men were wounded.

It was what passed for 'quiet' on the Western Front. The average kind of day when 300 men became casualties on the British side of their thirty-odd mile line.

It was a fine July evening and the men marched south-east out of Locon along what is now the Rue des Facons to the bigger road, the Route d'Armentieres. From the junction they marched east, passed by Le Touret, and two miles or so further on, turned right towards L'Epinette - there are many hamlets in Artois that share the name. Guides from the battalion they were relieving - the 8th Gordon Highlanders - met them. The Highlanders were, like Jim's King's Own Scottish Borderers, a unit of the 'new armies'. They'd been in France a day or two longer than Jim's battalion and had been the first of the new boys into the firing line.

The Highlanders' guides, three per platoon, some 48 officers and men in all, set out at 6 pm to meet the Borderers at the Brigade HQ some way to the rear of the front line trenches. The guides were then meant to lead the relieving troops via a place called Indian Village to the trenches dug into what had been an orchard; it was still called 'the Orchard' though that summer, the fruit trees that survived were stripped stumps. There the handover was to take place.

These handovers were meant to run like clockwork. Major North's *Trench Standing Orders* is clear on that. They rarely did.

A day before the relief, the incoming company and platoon commanders would inspect the trenches and take a briefing from the officers they were relieving. They'd have forms to fill in and sign off. Inventories of stores, supplies and ammunition. At more or less the same time, the battalion specialists - the snipers, signalers, machine gunners etc - would take over their new posts. This could be done in daylight - the main relief usually happened at night for safety. And for the same reason, it was supposed to take place under the strictest discipline. The relieving battalion would march the last few miles following their guides along pre-arranged routes, often along or beside communication trenches. They'd march in near silence. And no smoking. No lights at all.

The moment of handover was precisely choreographed. Platoon by platoon, the men of the battalion being relieved took up their positions on the fire step. Platoon by platoon, the men of the relief filed in behind them. Each man in turn along both lines in parallel would whisper the word 'pass'. The whisper would move along the line like a wave. And as each pair of men whispered, they passed. Changed places. When every man in the relieved battalion had passed, the relieved troops would march back company by company to rest billets or, if it was a time of high activity, the support trenches.

That was what the manual said. On this occasion, it was not the reality. On many occasions it was not.

First, the Borderers were half an hour late at the rendezvous. Then, one of B company's platoons lost touch with the rest of their company. Neither they nor their guides seem to have known how to remake contact. So they sat down by the side of the road and waited. Delay added to delay.

The lost platoon never did find the right route to the front and the handover was a mess. Both battalions' A and D companies did manage to change places by midnight. Jim was a member of D company which took up position in the support trenches.

The C companies did not change over until about 2.15 while the B companies did not do so until 3.45, by which time day was breaking. The lost Borderers had managed to find the front eventually. But they got there by the wrong communication trench. One man was wounded in the handover.

The Borderers settled into their new roles. For the company commander, the first hour or so was all about assuring himself that his men were in position, alert and ready. Sentries were posted and platoon commanders told precisely the section of front they were responsible for.

Every man had to have a position from which he could fire. Officers would need to be familiarised with the location of company HQs, the reserve ammunition and the latrines. And they'd have to pull together quickly, within 24 hours, a detailed report including a description of the field of fire, distance from the enemy and the general condition of their trenches and defences

Two of the most important routine duties were those of sentries and the watch. In daylight, there'd be one sentry for every three bays. By night or in poor visibility, one for every bay - though the final number and disposition was up to the battalion commander. Officers and NCOs took it in turns to be on watch, making hourly visits to all sentries, machine gun and bombing posts in their area.

For the men, every period of daylight began and ended in the same way. Stood-to. The men were stood-to an hour before daybreak and an hour before dark. In high summer, that would mean standing-to at about 3.30 am and again at about 9.30 pm. In the morning, they'd remain stood-to until the German lines were clearly visible. In the evening, until darkness fell. During these stand-tos, platoon commanders inspected the men's weapons and kit. They'd check each rifle's bolt action. They'd check ammunition, 120 rounds a man that would be made up to that number if the rifle had been fired. And they'd check the men's two gas masks, more usually called 'smoke helmets' in 1915.

Since the Germans had first used gas on the Western Front, at Ypres in April, helmet drill was a priority. The men were assured that the smoke helmets offered 'complete protection against all forms of gas used by the enemy'. If that were true at all, it was only in theory and in perfect conditions.

They were hard to put on, uncomfortable, restricted both vision and breathing and were only effective if the men got them on and secured before the gas reached them. But they were the only protection the men had and so time and again they practiced putting them on, adjusting them and taking them off.

Gas was most lethal when it took men by surprise. Early warning was the best defence. Wind direction and speed were closely watched and when either or both seemed to favour a gas attack, the order would go out to be on the alert. One of the sentries' duties was to look and smell for gas and they'd strike gongs or ring bells at the first sign. When that happened, every officer and man was to put on his helmet, secure it and make for his alarm post in the trench. As a back-up, men would pass the order 'put on smoke helmets' to those nearest to them.

It was assumed that gas was a prelude to an infantry attack. Standing orders said that when the enemy released gas, the artillery was to start up a bombardment directed at the section of enemy trench where the gas had been spotted. Machine gunners were then to focus intense fire in the same direction.

For every man, his rifle was the centre of his life. It had to work and had to be kept in good condition. There'd be those dawn and dusk inspections. Then another at midday. Ammunition would be checked over, too - dirty or defective bullets jammed rifles. At night, in fog or in snowstorms men had to fix bayonets and keep them fixed. And when there was gas, they had to work their rifle's moving parts to resist corrosion.

Men had a tricky call to make when it came to opening fire. The order was to shoot only if there was a clear target and not to do it indiscriminately. That could be punished. But if there was an attack, each man was expected to open rapid fire without waiting for orders.

If a sentry spotted an enemy working or reconnaissance party, he was to report it to the platoon commander who'd organise a sniper. Every battalion had a sniping section of about 64 NCOs and men. Their first duty was obvious - to pick off individual enemy soldiers. But they were also part of the battalion's intelligence operation. They were required to keep careful logs of numbers killed and wounded; position of enemy sniping posts; alterations in enemy trenches or wire; and any enemy activity.

At night, firing was even more strictly controlled. Both British and German patrols were likely to be out in no-man's-land, on reconnaissance or working on their wire or trenches. The risk of killing men from one's own side was high. Men were to open fire only if ordered to do so by a company commander who would first check on friendly patrols and try to make sure they were not shot. It did not always go to plan.

There'd be patrols most nights. The usual pattern was to detail two patrols, each made up of an NCO and three men who'd work half a night each. They'd go out and come back along specially designated zig-zag paths through the wire. Again, to offer some protection against friendly fire from British sentries - soldiers not on the zig-zag were considered enemy and could be fired on.

In theory, men's daily life in the trenches was to be little different from that in billets or in camp. They were expected to be washed, shaved and smartly dressed at midday inspection. Everyone except stretcher bearers had to carry their arms and equipment with them as they moved about the trenches. And moving meant marching 'correctly' under the eyes of an officer or NCO. Sleeping in the trenches was forbidden unless there was nowhere else. And no-one was to leave the trenches without permission.

Sentries were to stand at all times unless the trench parapet was too low to offer them protection. And they were not allowed to cover their ears, even in the freezing cold.

Cooking, eating, washing and shaving were all supposed to happen in the support trenches. Water, latrines and the rubbish of everyday life were constant problems, water, especially. Generally, there was too much of it but of the wrong kind. Either falling in torrents from the sky, flooding trenches and ditches, standing in pools or sluggish streams or leaching upwards from the water table. All of it, except the rainfall before it hit the earth, was heavily contaminated. At times, sentries were posted to stop men drinking it. Diarrhoea or dysentery could lay low dozens of men at a time.

Clean water was brought up each night in water carts and stored in the trenches in old rum jars and barrels. Or, if the men were unlucky, old petrol cans.

Latrines were built as far back from the trenches as practicable. For hygiene and safety, the further away the better. But it was always a compromise. Too far and men would relieve themselves in the trenches with all the hazards to health that entailed. Too close, and men could find themselves in danger at an exquisitely vulnerable moment. The British preferred to use buckets as latrines rather than limed pits and the aim was to empty and disinfect the buckets each night.

Perhaps Major North's manual did describe a kind of deep underlying structure of life in the trenches. But the reality was often different. There was constant activity behind the firing line even when, as in the mid-summer of 1915, it was described as "quiet". Congestion, confusion, misleading sketch maps, unreliable communication - all were threads in the imperfect weave of military life at the front. Add in the constant sniping, intermittent trench mortars, retaliation and counter-attacks and it's easy to see how the ideal was rarely the real.

Plus, maintaining discipline amongst a company's 250 or so young men, however well drilled, was never easy. They were not angels.

***

On the Borderers' first full day in the forward trenches, a German rifle grenade killed 3 men and wounded 3 more, all from 'A' company. It was a 'quiet' day.

While they were in the trenches, they worked on maintaining and improving them. But that work was hampered by the difficulty of getting materials up to the firing line. There was no option but to send out fatigue parties to carry supplies up. And telephone communication was less than ideal. The lines had been laid in a hurry, were badly protected and often broken.

Over the six days in this sector, two more men were killed and 20 wounded, one dying later of his injuries. On 15 July, they pulled back to the reserve trenches, relieved by the 11th Highland Light

Infantry. That battalion's war diary describes the handover in less than complimentary terms.

The Highlanders had spent the previous week, while the Borderers were in the trenches, repairing and strengthening garrisons and redoubts - in this case, fortified farm houses - behind the line. They got the order to make the relief on 12 July and marched up after dark on 14 July. Unfortunately, the Borderers failed to send out enough guides and it took far longer than expected to complete the handover. It was done by 2.30 a.m., fortunately without casualties.

Jim's battalion pulled back to the reserve trenches. With his customary reticence, Col Maclean tells us little of what the men did there for the following week. But it is almost certain that they picked up the Highlanders' jobs manning and working on garrisons and redoubts to the immediate rear of the line. One man in Jim's battalion was killed and three wounded, presumably by German field guns or trench mortars, on 19 July at No.1 Redoubt.

Pont d'Hinges today. The modern bridge can be seen in the distance

They left their work in the reserve trenches at 5 pm on 21 July and marched to billets near Pont d'Hinges, a tiny hamlet just west of Locon, by a bridge over the Canal d'Aire. In the two weeks in the trenches, 5 men had been killed outright. Twenty-three had been wounded, one dying later.

Pont d'Hinges was a billet far enough from the front for many battalions to find something resembling rest and recuperation, though drill, training and heavy work continued. Jim and his comrades spent the next nine days there, until the last day of July. Some were detailed to carry out fatigues at Le Touret. All had the opportunity to have a bath in the canal.

Drowning during these mass bathing sessions was not unknown. Few men could swim.

Towards the end of the battalion's time by the Canal d'Aire, its senior officers made another visit to the trenches to reconnoitre the next deployment.

***

The last day of July was mostly taken up with preparations to return to the trenches. Some time that day, Jim found time to write a postcard to his mother.

It provides one of the few days and dates in Jim's life for which we have any hard evidence.

The picture on Jim's card to his mother, written at Pont d'Hinges on 31 July 1915

> British. Exped. Force
> July 31st 1915
>
> Dear Mother
> Just a few lines on this card to let you know I have not forgotten you hoping this finds you well as it leaves me in the pink at present. This is not like I use cord I could not get another like that at the time. I will close now as they are coming for letters & I shall not get them off to day if I don't look sharp
> Love to all xxxxxxx
> Jim

This might well have been Jim's last card to his mother. It is short and like many cards home, says almost nothing. Except that he is worried about the picture on the other side.

It reads:

> *British Exped Force*
>
> *July 31st 1915*
>
> *Dear Mother,*
>
> *Just a few lines on this card to let you know I have not forgotten you hoping this finds you well as it leaves me in the pink at present. This is not like Ive's card I could not get another like that at the time. I will close now as they are coming for letters & I shall not get them off to day if I do not look sharp.*
>
> *Love to*
> *all*
>
> *xxxxxxxx*
>
> *Jim*

There is much to be read between these few terse lines. He seems anxious that he has not written as recently or as frequently as he might have done ... though finds it difficult to think of anything to say.

His anxiety seems to have been deepened by the lack of an appropriate card. It looks like he bought it at the last minute, something of an afterthought when his choices were limited. The picture on the card is not ideal, more suitable for a lover, fiancé or wife than a mother. And he is worried that it is not as good as the card he sent to his wife's younger sister, Ivy who he calls 'Ive'. It seems he thinks his mother might see that card and 'be vexed' that it's better, more carefully chosen. Perhaps a hint that his mother was in regular touch with his wife's family.

A second postcard of the three that survive he wrote to his wife, May - probably on the same day. This card is one of two that he sent her that day - the first is lost. His anxiety over his mother's card is still on his mind. It begins mid- sentence:

> *... so you can tell Ive I have wrote to him. I am sending her and mother a card each. Tell Mam not to be vexed because she has not got a good one. I could only get 2 at a time & I will send her a good one next time. Think this is all this time with all my love & kisses to you my dear wife and child from Your loving husband Jim*

*The front of one of just two surviving postcards
from Jim to his wife May.*

The text on Jim's postcard begins mid-way through a sentence. It seems to have been the second of two cards sent on that day.

Jim's choice of postcards seems rarely to have been ideal. This chin-jutting, military image is a contrast to the warm message on its back.

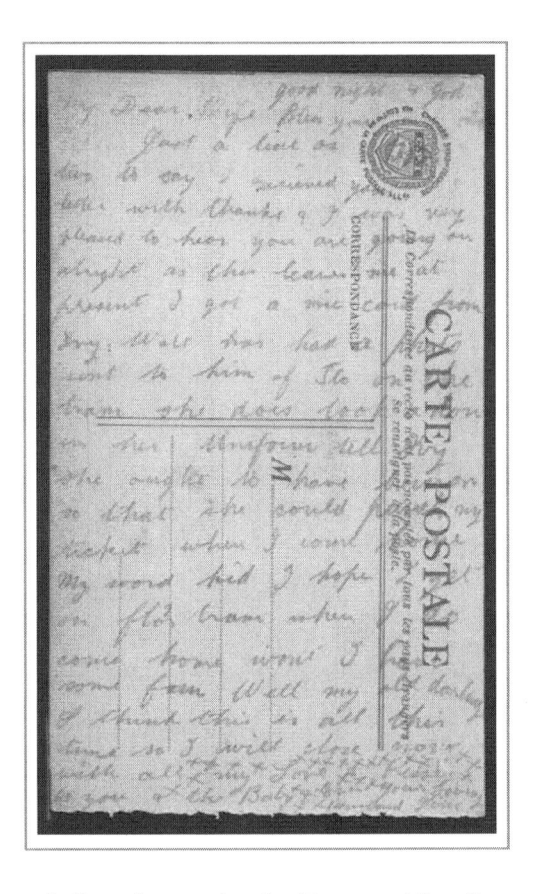

Sadly, we have no date for this postcard from Jim to his wife. Nor do we know how many like this he sent nor of any that he received.

> *PS Tell Ivy I will look out for her Cake & thank her from me*

We do not know who the 'he' is nor why Ivy needs to know Jim has written to him. Perhaps one of his brothers in law. He asks May to speak to his mother to excuse his choice of card - 'not ... a good one'. That again suggests his mother and his wife might speak as a matter of course, perhaps because they were neighbours. And there was the promised cake. Ivy seems to have written regularly to Jim and he to her.

Just one more of Jim's postcards survives. Written to May. It is wordier than the others and its tone lighter. But it is impossible to date.

> *My Dear Wife,*
>
> *Just a line or two to say I received your letter with thanks & I was very pleased to hear you are going on alright as this leaves me at present. I got a nice card from Ivy. Walt has had a photo sent to him of Flo on the tram. She does look a ???? in her uniform tell Ivy she ought to have been on so that she could punch my ticket when I come home*

My word kid I hope I get on Flo's tram when I do come home won't I have some fun. Well my old darling I think this is all this time so I will close now

with all my love to you and the Baby. Kisses from your loving husband Jim.

Once again, we see that his sister in law, Ivy, has written. And there is the little vignette of his friend's wife who had started working on the Doncaster trams. 'Walt' was Walter Shickel. 'Flo', his wife, was May's eldest sister. They lived next door to May in one of the houses in the Johnson compound. Walt was several years older than Jim but they'd signed up at the same time and were now serving together in the same battalion, almost certainly the same company and platoon.

***

By 1 am on 1 August, Jim and his battalion were back in the front trenches, once again in the sector to the east of Festubert. We have a good description of these trenches, not from the 6th Borderers' own battalion diary but from that of the 11th Highland Light Infantry who relieved them on 8 August.

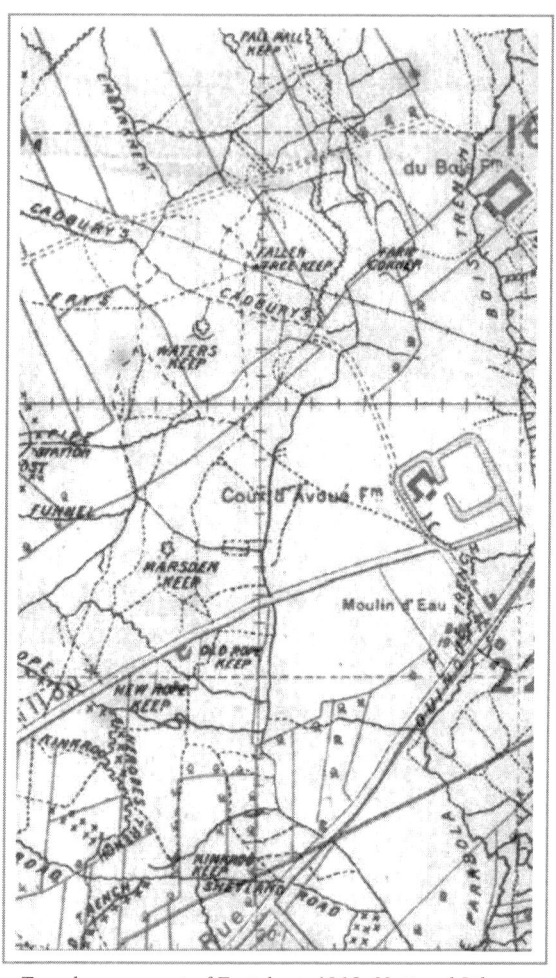

Trench map - east of Festubert, 1915 (National Library of Scotland)

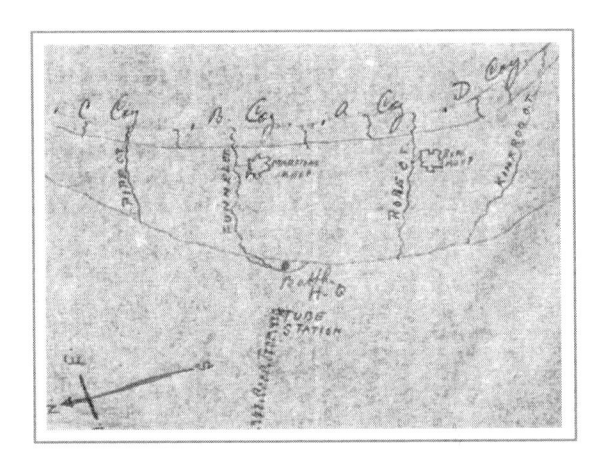

Sketch map of the stretch of trenches near Festubert, occupied by the 6th KOSB on their second deployment to the front line. (Map opposite). It shows the position of the companies of the 11th HLI. (National Archives)

The section lay between two communication trenches; 'Pipe' at the the northern end, 'Kink Roo' at the southern end - the odd name was the British soldiers' pronunciation of Quinque Rue, a small road and, before the war, cluster of houses in the area. Today, the site of the trench lies along a line that runs for a mile or so south from Richebourg L'Avoue to the Rue de Lille east of Festubert.

One of the distinctive features of this stretch of the line was the wooden railway that brought up supplies and rations from the railhead to the north west. Fatigue parties had laid wooden rails in a dead straight line to a depot close by by battalion HQ called 'Tube Station'. The men called it the 'Kink Roo' or 'King's Road' tramway. Wooden wagons were manhandled up and down the tramway - hard work but much better than hauling heavy supplies on road wagons up to their axles in mud. Inevitably, though, the wooden rails would warp, buckle and snap. And the wagons were always coming off the rails and had to be lugged back. Nor could it carry the really heavy stuff - building materials for the Royal Engineers for example. That still had to be carried by fatigue parties.

Clean water was in reasonable supply. There was one pump at HQ and another at Dead Cow Farm, both just behind the line. The downside was that the old petrol cans the men used to take water up to the firing trench were not always as fragrant as they might have been.

In general, the trenches in this sector were in better condition than those the Borderers had occupied earlier. But there was always work to be done; strengthening the parapet with earth dug from a pit in front of the trench; wire to be repaired and thickened; dugouts to be rebuilt and strengthened. And in parts of this sector, there was the relative luxury of a brick floor in the main trenches. It was a boon in the torrential rain of the first three days of August.

The battalion spent a week in these front line trenches, receiving a new contingent of 50 men that brought it almost up to full strength - 29 officers and 984 men. Sniping was frequent. Trench mortars crashed down, apparently at random. Casualties, though, were lighter than before and on the night of 8/9 August they were relieved by the 11th Highland Light Infantry.

For the next week, the battalion was in the reserve trenches. Once again, they were kept hard at work building and repairing garrisons and redoubts.

And it was while they were there, on August 14 1915, that back in Yorkshire, May's mother, Ellen, died. She was just 55 years old. We do not know whether or when May wrote to Jim to tell him. Or how he received the news. What he replied. It is hard to believe it was without pain.

After that week in the reserve trenches, they were relieved at 9 pm on 17 August and marched first to bivouac near Les Choquaux, a tiny hamlet south west of Locon close to the Canal d'Aire. The following morning, at 7.30, they paraded and marched to rest billets in Le Cornet Bourdois - a welcome break well behind the front line, close to the battalion's previous billets in Bourecq and Guarbecque. The village, remarkably, had an oyster bar in a wine shop and a female barber. She was very popular.

It was while Jim and his battalion were in Le Cornet that Kitchener made it clear to Haig that a mass British infantry attack at Loos was non-negotiable. That he must find a way to do whatever Joffre demanded. There would be a British assault on German lines south of the La Bassée canal around Loos. Jim would be part of it.

***

At 6.30 am on the morning of the 31 August, the men paraded and marched to Verquin, a small town south of Bethune. They stayed one night. At 2 pm on the following day, 1 September, they marched to their new front line trenches just south of the La

Bassée canal, in front of Cambrin. They arrived at 7 pm and took over their new positions.

The weather broke. It rained almost continuously for the next seven days. The temperature fell, too. Autumn. But it was once again a 'quiet' week in the trenches. A mere handful of men died or were maimed.

On the night of 6/7 September, the 11th Royal Scots relieved the Borderers who pulled back to rest billets in Vendin les Bethune. They had just three days to recover there before returning to the reserve lines, this time near Annequin, a little to the south of their previous positions. On 15 September, at 8 am, they left the reserve trenches and moved up to the front line.

By now, the battalions who were to take part in the Loos offensive were beginning to prepare in earnest. While Haig was keen to keep the plan to use gas a semi-secret, it could not be kept from the men at the front, some of whom were tasked with building emplacements for the cylinders. Others had been detailed to act as guides for the gas carrying parties - and they toured the trenches to mark out the positions to which they would supervise delivery.

When the Borderers went back into the front line this time, it was into the trenches they would occupy on the morning of 25 September, the first day of the Battle of Loos. They faced Auchy les Mines, or Auchy les La Bassée (sic) as it was sometimes called, astride the road from Vermelles to Auchy and to the south of the railway line.

They faced some of the toughest places in the German line; the formidable Hohenzollern Redoubt to their right. A heavily fortified machine gun post called Mad Point straight ahead.

The sniping from the German strongpoints was incessant and shells fell almost without pause on the Borderers' rear. On 19 September, the men watched a plume of smoke rise high into the air from the Hohenzollern Redoubt. A massive explosion, cause unknown.

Another 'quiet' week.

***

For the British generals, September was all about planning for a battle none wanted.

Haig remained sceptical about the ground. There were some advantages but not many. The attack would be along a broad front, from the canal in the north to the outskirts of Loos in the south. And the broader the front, the less chance the enemy had to attack the infantry's flanks. Many of the troops that would be committed to the battle were relatively fresh, well-trained and well-prepared. The 'new armies' who'd had enough of a taste of trench warfare to ready them for the battle.

But he still did not have the guns or shells to mount the intense, lengthy, destructive bombardment he and his senior officers knew was an absolute prerequisite for a successful infantry attack. As summer had turned to autumn, gas had fixed itself in his mind as the only viable way to make up for his artillery shortfall.

When Haig first met the sappers' gas expert, Colonel Foulkes, in July, he thought gas might have a military use if it could be deployed with surprise and on a grand scale - his preference was for the five mile front facing Aubers Ridge. But any thoughts he might have had of a new attack in that sector, with or without gas, were brought to an abrupt halt on 19 August when Kitchener effectively ordered him to get on with planning to do whatever the French asked him to. That meant an attack over the ground near Loos that he'd already judged unsuitable.

When Haig met Colonel Foulkes again, on 21 August, he asked whether it would be possible to supply enough chlorine for 6300 yards of front - about three and half miles - by 15 September, the notional date of the Loos attack. Colonel Foulkes assured him that was possible - indeed, he could have that amount now; much more by mid-September. The following day, Thursday 22 August Haig drove north to a field in the British training area near St Omer to watch a demonstration. Not just chlorine gas but a variety of smoke bombs and grenades designed to obscure and protect the infantry's flanks.

He was persuaded.

***

The last few days of August and beginning of September, though, were frustrating. The plant producing the gas had fallen below expectations and only half of what had been promised was now expected by 4 September. Colonel Foulkes advised that either the attack should be postponed or the front narrowed. That was the last thing Haig would consider - he knew a broad front was essential and that he needed enough gas for the biggest possible simultaneous release, to make the most of the element of surprise.

On 2 September, news came that the plant had broken down again. Haig asked for and got an assurance that he would have enough come the day. Two days later, on Saturday 4 September, that prospect improved - though for unsettling reasons - when the French postponed the attack ten days. The new date was 25 September.

Haig was unsettled at the news because his plan depended on surprise. Intelligence suggested the Germans were not expecting gas. Not at the moment, at least. Their machine gunners had only rudimentary gas masks. With delay came the risk that the enemy would learn about the planned gas attack and issue their men with better protection.

Haig became obsessed with secrecy. So much so that when the first gas cylinders arrived at Bethune station on 4 September, he sent them back to Boulogne and the specialist gas companies, the men who would open the taps, back to St Omer. He feared that if the specialists mixed with the 'other' troops, the secret might leak out. It was an odd precaution to take. Only a few days later, men in the front line trenches were ordered to build gas emplacements and to work out how they would ferry the cylinders up to the front.

Haig was both unsettled and obsessed by the weather. The strength and direction of the wind was the most important factor in a gas attack. That meant preparing for two possibilities: that wind would be ideal or that it would be from the wrong direction or too light. It also meant uncertainty over which plan would be put into action until perhaps minutes before any attack had to be launched.

With nine days to go, on Thursday 16 September, Haig met his Corps Commanders, Generals Rawlinson and Gough, and put the blunt question to them: 'if we have to attack on the 25th without gas, what modifications will it be necessary to make to your plans?' Both said they would have to narrow the line and attack only the enemy salients - the Hohenzollern Redoubt and the bulge around Loos itself.

Haig knew this 'plan within a plan' had no chance of success, no chance of avoiding mass slaughter and no chance of offering any real support for the French offensive further south. But it stayed on the table until the moment the gas taps were opened at ten to six on the morning of 25 September.

Not everyone in the British High Command was as persuaded as Haig about the use of gas. Sir Henry Robertson, the BEF's Chief of Staff, wrote to Haig saying he found the decision to use gas a 'difficult' one. Haig replied sharply that he did not understand the difficulty. With gas "decisive results were to be expected"; without gas "the fronts of attack must be restricted, with the result of concentrated hostile fire on the attacking troops". "The attack ought not to be launched", he concluded, "except with the use of gas".

Robertson's doubts were only one frustration for Haig, however. With a little over a week to go to the offensive, Haig found out that too few cylinders were being delivered. He urged Robertson to set his 'difficulties' aside and to send an officer to the plant in England to force them to work 24 hour shifts.

A week to go, Haig talked Sir John French through his plans. As he had predicted, he had the heavy guns and shells to support an attack by two divisions on one or two narrow fronts, an attack that could get nowhere. Add gas and he could attack with six divisions along the whole Loos front. That was why, he explained to Sir John, that, weather permitting, he had to use gas.

It is not clear how much of the briefing Sir John absorbed. His many sicknesses and fevers over that summer meant Sir John often took to his bed. And when his mind was not on his own health, its frequent changes mystified and frustrated those around him. There is alarming evidence that, at crucial moments, the most senior British officer in France, the Commander in Chief of the Expeditionary Force, was not always mentally present. His conduct over the matter of reserves is a case in point.

Haig had come to understand that in trench warfare, the first attack had to push as far and fast as possible. And any success in breaking through the German line had to be followed up almost instantly. Flooding reserves into the battle at the points the enemy seemed weakest. Each of his corps commanders would have their own men in close reserves. But the General Reserve was not under

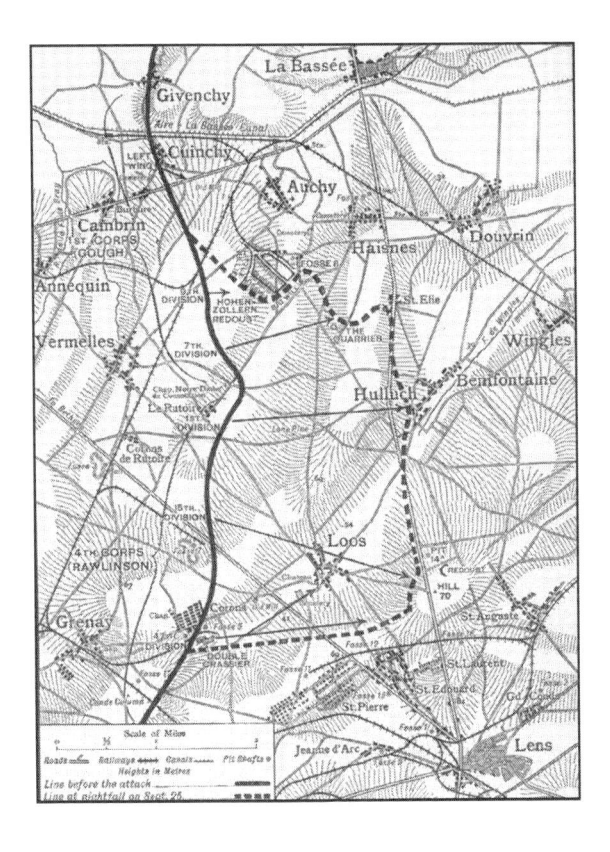

The Battle of Loos. The thick line is the British position on the morning of battle. The dotted line, the position at the end of the first day

Haig's or his subordinates' command. It came under GHQ and followed the orders of Sir John French.

Haig wanted the General Reserve waiting at Noeux les Mines and Verquin by the morning of the battle, half a dozen miles from the front line. Sir John thought that was too close. He intended to bring up the General Reserve only as far as Lillers, some fifteen miles from the battle, and then not until 24 September, the eve of the battle. "This is too late", Haig thundered.

It is far from clear what picture of the coming battle Sir John had in his mind. Nor how much he knew or understood of what was happening around him. When he wrote his account of the Battle of Loos in a dispatch published in the London Gazette in November 1915, little of it concurred with reality. His main purpose was to justify his own incomprehensible decisions and actions. A futile apologia - he was sacked, replaced by Haig, at the end of the year.

***

On 21 September, the British artillery began a four day, and four night, bombardment. The precursor to the infantry advance, now fixed for the morning of 25 September. As the bigs guns opened, Jim's battalion moved back to the reserve trenches where it spent the next three days watching. And waiting.

Two days into the bombardment, on Thursday 24 September, just 36 hours before the infantry was due to go in, Sir John's Chief of Staff, Sir William Robertson, met Haig for lunch. They discussed the chilling realisation that Sir John:

> *"does not realise the size of the units (with) which he is fighting the forthcoming battle".*

He seemed to think only three divisions would be involved in the battle - about 36,000 men - along with two cavalry corps in reserve, "when really" Haig wrote, "he is fighting with 3 Armies and 2 Cavalry Corps!!"

At least he was right about the size of the reserve. But his blinkered focus on those reserves and his stubbornness over how they should be used was to prove fatal.

To the plan and to thousands of men.

Saturday 25 September 1915

It is 5 am. The rain of the past two days, at times torrential, has eased to a thick drizzle. The earth is sodden. Water lies in pools in the pocks and tracks in the open land. It covers the bottom of the trenches. It is ankle deep. There is barely any wind.

There is no silence. For almost 100 hours, British guns have tossed tons of high explosives and shrapnel onto German lines. Those lines are no more than 400 yards from where Lance Corporal James Airton is standing. Sitting. Leaning. Talking. Waiting.

It is 5 am and no-one knows what is to happen next.

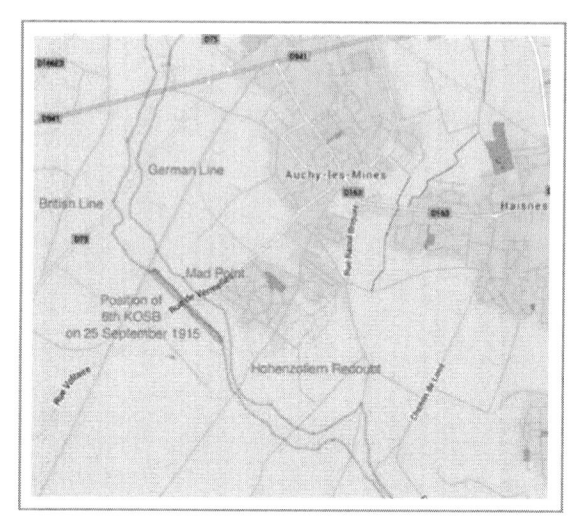

The approximate position of the 6th KOSB on a modern map.

Perhaps the first plan. Perhaps they will release thousands of tons of chlorine gas into the still, damp air. The 'utility'. The 'accessory'. Perhaps a five mile line of 60,000 men will rise as one out of the trenches to charge and slide and slip and fall in the dense clay.

Perhaps the other plan. There are two plans. Perhaps they will not let the gas go. Perhaps just 20,000 men will do what they can along a shortened line of two miles or so. Their flanks naked to the

German machine gunners. Knowing they cannot do what their orders say they must.

It is 5 am and the biggest infantry battle in the history of Europe is perhaps an hour and a half away. Or perhaps it is not. Perhaps it will not happen at all.

Jim and the rest of the 6th Battalion of the King's Own Scottish Borderers have been back in the front line trenches for less than 24 hours. For the three days before that, they'd waited in the reserve trenches near a small town called Annequin.

There, they'd watched and heard and felt the rhythmic hammer blows of what was meant to be a crippling artillery bombardment. One that, their officers have told them, will destroy the German wire. Demoralise the German troops. Disable their machine guns.

It is 5 am. Now they are in the front line. Waiting. If they are to go, theirs will be the hardest task in this unwanted battle.

Jim and his battalion hold the section of trench that cuts the road from Vermelles to Auchy Les

Today: towards Mad Point.

Today: towards Hohenzollern Redoubt

Mines. Or what remains of them. A man foolish enough to peer over the parapet would look north east. Some 400 yards away, the German front line trench. The Madagascar Trench.

They had been here, or very near here, twice before.

Straight ahead, the battalion's first obstacle and objective. 'Mad Point'. A machine gun post that controls the Vermelles-Auchy road and stands in front of the remnants of Madagascar village, the Corons de Maroc and Corons de Pekin. Their exotic names belie their drab reality. Smashed shells of what were once rows of miners' terraced houses.

To their right, one of the strongest strongpoints of the German front. The Hohenzollern Redoubt. It bulges 600 yards from the German line. Its nose no more than 250 yards from the British line. It is a fortress with innards of steel and concrete driven onto and into a low slagheap that for all its modest height dominates the low, flat, sodden land around. Its surface a bristling skin of half buried machine guns. They have an uninterrupted, 270 degree field of fire. Behind them, a rash of trenches speed ammunition and reserves to the front. No-man's land here is "as nasty a bit of ground as any on the battlefield".

It is the job of two battalions to take the redoubt – the 5th Cameron Highlanders and the 7th Seaforths. Whatever the speed of their success or failure, German machine gunners on the western face of the redoubt will fix their sights at the flanks of the 6th King's Own Scottish Borderers.

A German sap trench - a spur sticking out into no-man's-land from the main 'Little Willie' trench - called 'Strong Point' along with 'Mad Point' forms a lethal amphitheatre. The Borderers' script say this is where they must make their entrance. And when that act is over, when they're through the German line, they will fight building by building from miner's house to miner's, pit shed to pit shed, over railway tracks and low slagheaps:

> "a ghoulish type of village warfare, in which direction would tend to be lost … (with) congestion at one place and gaps at another … "

Their orders are ambitious. Their objectives are way beyond the points Strong and Mad. The town hall clocks of Haisnes and Douvrin. Haisnes is to be taken quickly, even though it is a good two miles away.

It is 5 am and no-one knows what is to happen next. It depends on the wind. Partly on the wind.

Gas is a gamble. A grim game. An aetherial game of chance. Gas debilitates, demoralises and destroys. It destroys, burns and corrodes men and machines. But it can not be aimed. It is the caprice of nature that decides whether it kills, blinds or burns your own men or the enemy. The strength and direction of the wind. The only moment of human control is the moment of decision. Whether to open them or not.

It is 5 am. Jim waits. Waits for that decision and all that will follow.

Gas can not do all that artillery can. It can not uproot and cut the tangles of barbed wire that slow or halt an advancing soldier. Force each man into a high-stepping, macabre dance. Turn him into a standing target. Nor can it excavate the booby traps, the pits lined with spikes.

If the the day goes well and the men advance quickly, they will likely meet 'friendly' gas as well as hostile men and guns in the enemy trenches.

At 2 pm the day before, the Commander of the British Expeditionary Force's First Army, General Douglas Haig, had held a brief conference with his Corps Commanders, Generals Rawlinson and Gough. They went over the plan and the 'plan within a plan' once again. If the wind was favourable, the order would go out to release the gas twenty minutes after 'zero hour', coinciding with an artillery climax. Forty minutes after that, the infantry would lift from their trenches in an unbroken line, five or six miles long, from the La Bassée canal in the north to the Loos salient in the south. A diversionary attack from Givenchy, north of the canal, would begin three hours before the main assault. Notionally, at 3.30 am.

If it were not possible to use gas, then General Gough was to attack the Hohenzollern Redoubt at 3.30 am. General Rawlinson was to attack the Loos salient at the same time as the French army to his right, an attack that would not begin before 10 am.

Haig said he would let them know by 10 pm that evening which plan it would be. The final decision, though, was not his. It was nature's. The wind. And his weather expert, Ernest Gold, was not encouraging.

After that eve of battle conference, Haig went out on horseback to look over the battlefield that shook under blast after blast of ton after ton of high explosive. He was anxious. About those things he could control and those things he could not. The enemy. The men's readiness. The wind.

By early evening, the weather reports had seemed favourable. Just.

Then, at 9.20 pm, the 24 hour forecast came in. "Wind southerly then changing to southwest or west, probably increasing to 20 miles per hour". A 20 mph westerly wind would have been ideal. A southwesterly at the same speed, less than ideal but still possible. A southerly at any strength would be a disaster. Most of the British line ran north-south and any wind on that bearing would take the gas from one section of British trench to another.

It was not the best forecast but on the strength of it, Haig ordered the men into the assembly and fire trenches. He walked outside. The wind "seemed from the southwest but very light". He spent the next hours:

> *"wondering what the wind would be in the morning. The greatest battle in the world's history begins today – some 800,000 French and British troops will actually attack today."*

At 2 am, the wind had fallen to no more than a breath. Time was running out. The tunnelers near Givenchy needed 2½ hours notice of zero hour to prepare and explode their underground mine.

At 3 am, the wind had fallen further. To about 1 mph. To all intents and purposes a dead calm. Haig's weather forecaster seemed paralysed by his science. Or its consequences. At this critical moment, he told Haig he could:

> *"not say anything definitely beyond that the wind would probably be stronger just after sunrise (5.30) than later in the day"*

It was the last possible moment to decide which order to give. If the weather forecast suggested anything, it was to hold back the gas. Haig ignored it. Fixed 'zero hour' for 5.30 am. That meant letting the gas go at 5.50 am, the main attack forty minutes later at 6.30 am.

But that was not the end of uncertainty.

It is 5 am. Thirty minutes to 'zero hour'. Fifty to the moment the gas taps open. Haig goes outside. One of his colleagues lights a cigarette. The smoke drifts "in puffs" towards the north east. It is "almost a calm". He orders Staff Officers to stand by. Even now, this close to 'zero hour' he might countermand the attack. For a quarter of an hour, he thinks. The lives of 60,000 British men hang in the balance:

> *"I feared the gas would simply hang about our trenches …"*

The decision is weighty. Science and reason tell him not to use the gas. They tell him gas will harm his own men as much as the enemy. That it will not reach the German machine gunners. It will not silence them. It will be another futile slaughter. Without gas, though, he is left with a smaller attack that is certain to fail. And will do nothing other than confirm French suspicions that the British were never committed to this 'big push'.

It is 5.15 am.

Haig gives the order. 'Carry on'. He climbs a wooden lookout tower.

It is 5.40. Haig persuades himself the wind is stronger. The leaves of a poplar tree whisper in the lightest of breezes. It is, he decides, 'satisfactory':

> " ... *but what a risk I must run of gas blowing back upon our dense mass of troops*"

At the northern end of the line, next to the La Bassée canal, facing Auchy les Mines, the air is still.

One of the men whose job it is to release the gas hesitates. Later, he recalled.

> *"The wind was now practically nil and it was drizzling, so on receipt of 'zero hour' only one hour before it was due I rang up 5th Brigade HQ and asked them if this meant I was to carry on. They said "yes, why?" I explained that I had reported unfavourably on the wind all night and would not hold myself responsible for the effect of gas on our own men ... I received the order to carry on".*

Another man, a senior officer, hesitates, too. He wants to stop the release. He calls Divisional HQ. He tells General Horne:

"The wind is unfavourable and I don't think I should release",

Horne is firm:

"The order is to turn on the gas"

The officer tells General Horne that the man whose job it is to turn on the tap is refusing to do it.

Hornes' final words are curt:

"Then shoot the bastard".

It is 5.50 am. The taps open. In Jim's trench, it is as bad as could be. The wind has backed. It is now a gentle south-easterly. The gas and the smoke waft back into the faces of the men waiting in the front line. Most, not all, pull their smoke helmets over their faces.

They wait. Until the time.

It is 6.30 am. The gas has drifted and now it is to their rear. Its only casualties here facing Auchy les Mines are British. Some from the gas that has been released. Some from a lucky strike German gunners made on some gas cylinders.

German heavy guns are shelling British trenches. Men are killed and wounded as they wait. One casualty is Colonel Maclean, the Commanding Officer of Jim's battalion.

It is 6.30 am. A and B Company of the 6th KOSB are ready. They will be the first to go. C and D - Jim's Company - will follow.

It is 6.30 am. The noise is unbearable. However much we try we can not imagine it or anything like it today. The closest is an intense spell of sheet lightning but that is a pale, temporary imitation.

There is the smell of wet earth. Of shit and rot and death. Of burnt explosives. Of smoke and gas.

It is 6.30 am. Whistles blow. Along the five miles of the line. Their shrill soprano cuts through the basso profundo of both sides' bombardments . The first of 60,000 men heave themselves, their half hundredweight packs, their rifles, wire cutters, spades and other kit over the parapets and out into no-man's-land.

It is 6.30 am. Pipe Major Robert Mackenzie hears the whistles. He waits in the centre of the Borderers' trench. He is 60 years old. At least 60 years old. Perhaps more. No-one knows for sure. He is a legend. He breathes deeply and blows hard into his chanter. Once, Twice. Again. The drones wake. He rises with the first men. Steps over parapet and into the open. His fingers pick out the tune. Men pass him and stride towards Mad Point. He is hit. He plays. He is hit. He plays and walks until bullet after bullet smashes his legs from under him. The German machine gunners are aiming at his pipes. He stops. He can go no further. He is dragged back.

Pipe Major McKenzie's wounds will kill him. He will be awarded the Victoria Cross.

It is a little after 6.30 am. The first two companies disappear into the fog and smoke. Some is from the British smoke candles. The rest from the German artillery barrage.

The second wave, including Jim's D Company, take their places in the front line trenches. They can not see what is happening in front of them. No news comes back from the men in front. No orders come from the rear. In the noise and smoke and confusion, no-one knows what has happened to their commanding officer, Major Maclean. The battalion's second in command, Major Hosley, decides to lead the second wave out of the trenches. To follow where he thinks the first has gone.

The author and journalist Arthur Conan Doyle described those first few moments of the attack like this:

"Nineteen officers led the Borderers over the parapet.

Within a few minutes the whole nineteen, including Colonel Maclean and Major Hosley, lay dead or wounded upon the ground. Valour could go no further."

The laconic battalion diary records those first moments like this:

"Battalion assaulted German trenches at MAD POINT & SE of MADAGASCAR trench at 6.30 am. The position was reached and at some points entered. Severe machine gun fire chiefly from flanks, undestroyed obstacles and uncertain effects of gas caused severe losses and prevented the attack from succeeding."

Some in that first wave, the first two companies, reach the German wire. It is intact. Untouched by four days of artillery bombardment. Worse, in front of the wire the men find that German engineers have cut an eight foot wide ditch. It is filled with stakes and barbed wire and covered over with loose turf.

The wire and the booby trap are holding up the men. Those behind, those in the second wave, catch up. They are bunched now, close to the wire. The German machine guns at Strong Point open up. Conan Doyle described it like this:

> *"Every accumulation of evil which can appall the stoutest heart was heaped upon this brigade ... the gas hung thickly about the trenches, and all the troops ... suffered from it ... The chief cause of the slaughter, however, was the uncut wire, which held up the brigade while the German rifle and machine-gun fire shot them down in heaps."*

Some struggle back to their trenches. A handful. Nine officers remain of the 29 who began the day. Of the men, some 300 still stand of the 924 who stood-to just before dawn. Lance Corporal James

Airton is not among those still standing. He is one of the 630 men killed, wounded, gassed or missing.

***

Exactly how, when or where James Airton died, we can never know.

There is a family story. It may or may not be true. Jim had joined up soon after the start of the war with his friend and neighbour, Walter Shickel. They trained together and fought together at Loos.

Walt survived the battle and, after the war, told how he'd been at Jim's side when he died. That they had gone over together. That he was talking to Jim at the moment he was hit. Shouting, more likely. Shouting over the noise. Perhaps they were standing. Perhaps walking or running. Walt said that Jim was hit by a shell or a trench mortar. And that he was blown to pieces while Walt himself was untouched.

We cannot know whether there is any truth in Walt's account. There is no reason to doubt it. Nor any to believe it.

***

The day is not over.

There is a second, failed attack in the late morning. Then it is afternoon. And the scraps of the 6th KOSB can do little more than help the 11th Highland Light Infantry pick up what they can of the dead and wounded.

It begins to rain. Heavy rain.

There are no words. Or if there are, they are few.

Captain Stair Gillon, an officer of the King's Own Scottish Borderers, had these a dozen years after that morning's slaughter.

> *"It was all over in a few minutes. The wonderful product of months of zeal, energy, and patriotism was 'knocked out' without opportunity of doing more than set an example to posterity by their bravery."*

***

The Battle of Loos was not finished on 25 September 1915, though it may as well have been.

By the first evening, the generals concluded from their observation towers that the day had gone well. Though at devastating cost.

Haig wrote that it had been:

> *" ... a very satisfactory one on the whole. We have captured 8,000 yards of German front, and advanced in places 2 miles from our old front line. This is the largest advance made on the Western Front since this kind of warfare started."*

It was a ghost of an advance. Over the next two days it became clear that while British troops had broken *into* the German lines, including those on and around the formidable Hohenzollern Redoubt, they had not broken *through* them.

That night, 25/26 September, the torrential rain continued. Communications were chaotic. Reserves were too far back or in the wrong place. Those that made it to the front were exhausted after lengthy forced marches. The Germans, by contrast, brought up their reserves quickly, over much shorter distances.

By the end of September, the Germans had counter-attacked and recaptured most of what they had lost that first day. And what they did not recapture then, they steadily clawed back over the first weeks of October.

The 'big push' had gone nowhere. By 12 October, the Allied High Command had to concede, if only to one another, that the French would be unable to advance beyond Vimy Ridge and the British would be unable to achieve the ambitious objectives the French had set for them.

The last major offensive of the Loos campaign of autumn 1915, on 13 October, was a pointless gesture. Casualties criminally high.

In one battalion, every single officer and man was hit by German machine gunners. In another, just one officer and one man reached their objective. In one Division 180 officers and almost 3,600 men were cut down in just ten minutes without gaining an inch of ground.

By 16 October, the balance sheet was scarcely credible. No breakthrough. No German retreat from French territory. Ground gained measured in feet and inches. At the price of 50,000 men dead, missing or wounded - almost 8,000 of them dead. The loss of 2,000 officers was to have consequences for the whole of the rest of the war.

Jim's battalion, the 6th KOSB, was one of those that suffered most. Six hundred and eighty were lost,

20 of them officers. By St Crispin's day, the five hundredth anniversary of the Battle of Agincourt, it was a battalion in name only.

KOSB Captain Stair Gillon wrote:

> *"We may marvel at the sanguine notion that the expenditure of a lavish, but impoverishing, gun-fire in a four days' preliminary bombardment, combined with the use of gas in its experimental stages at the hour of assault, would result in the breaching of the Germans' two systems of field fortifications - the gaining of the open country and a triumphant reunion with equally victorious French troops, somewhere between Valenciennes and Maubeuge, which would have vast strategic consequences."*

***

Nothing of Jim was ever found.

Epilogue

May, Jim's wife, knew nothing about the battle of Loos. Not at the time. Almost certainly, she would not have known her husband was even involved. Letters home did not give military secrets away. And until a few days, perhaps hours, before Jim went into the front line trenches for the last time, even he probably did not know the scale of what was to happen.

For the rest of September and October, May continued to write to him. None of her letters survive. But we do know that they were returned. Stamped brutally with the words 'Present Location Unknown'.

On at least one, a bureaucratic hand had written 'In Hospital'. An unintended deception, casual in its cruelty.

We cannot imagine her anxiety or that of the many young wives who every day would see in the local paper the names and sometimes photographs of men dead and missing on the Western Front. May read them looking for news. Hoping.

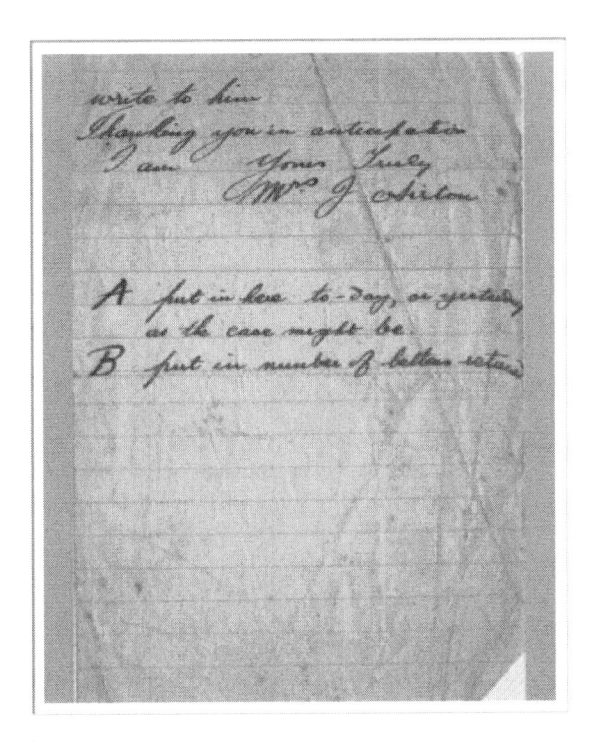

In late October or early November 1915, she decided to write to the War Office to ask for news. Among her few surviving papers is what seems to be a letter drafted for her, a pro forma. A letter to authority was a formidable task for a young woman brought up in an age of deference. Even for one who was confident in her careful copperplate script.

The letter composed for her reads:

Dear Sirs,

I have received back (A) *from the G.P.O (B) letters addressed to my husband Lance Corp J Airton No17269 15th Platoon, D Company 6th Battalion King's Own Scottish Borderers and they have been endorsed, in hospital, and also stamped Present Location Uncertain R.L.S L.P.S G.P.O, on the back of envelope (sic).*

Would you please cause enquiries to be made as to his whereabouts, and whether he is ill or wounded, so that I can write to him.

Thanking you in anticipation.

I am Yours Truly

Mrs J Airton

(A) put in here today or yesterday as the case may be

(B) put in number of letters returned

We do not know whether May ever put the letter into her own hand. And if she did, whether she posted it. We can imagine, however, the little effect it might have had.

In the first week of November, she received a letter from the Infantry Record Office telling her that her husband had been posted as "missing" after an engagement on 25/9/15. The letter included no information about where the engagement had taken place. Nor did it give any indication of where he might be.

May feared the worst. But still hoped he would be found. Turn up wounded. Lost, perhaps, in some hospital's bureaucracy.

On New Year's Day 1916, Alice Hurst, Jim's older sister, wrote to May:

> *Dear May,*
>
> *Best wishes for a happy new year and the Baby. Hope you will hear from Jim soon. I seem to think we shall ve(ry) soon.*
>
> *Love to the baby*
>
> *and accept some yourself*
>
> *from Alice*

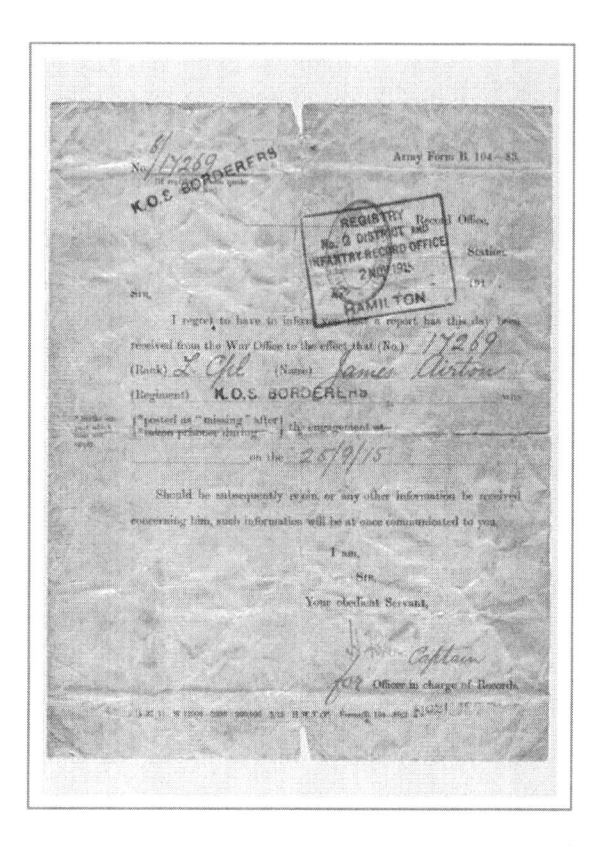

Weeks passed with no news. Then, on 19 May 1916, almost 8 months after Jim's death, the War Office wrote to May.

It was a letter that told her in the most brutal terms that she should not expect her husband back.

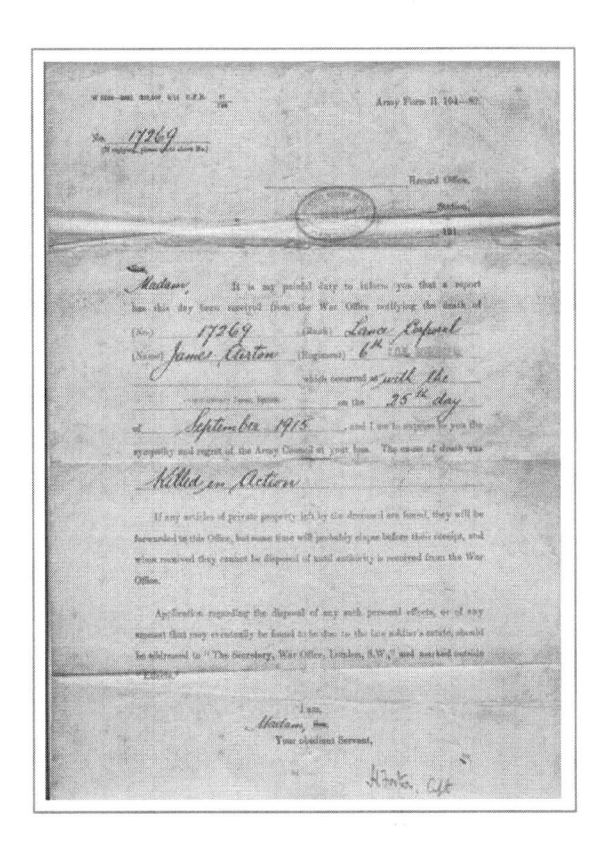

That her separation allowance of 17/6 (87.5p) a week, the money she'd been paid since her husband went to France, was to end on 4 June.

It would be replaced by a pension of 15/- (75p) a week.

The letter said the change of payment "must not be taken as indicating that there is any proof of the death of your husband". But it was clear that was what it meant.

A week later, on 25 May 1916, the Infantry Record Office wrote to tell May that:

> "*a report has been received this day from the War Office notifying the death of no 17269, Lance Corporal James Airton, 6th KOS Borderers which occurred with the Expeditionary Force, France on the 25th day of September 1915 ... The cause of death was killed in action*"

A month later, on 26 June, the War Office authorised a payment of £3 5s 7d (about £3.28p) to May as Jim's "sole legatee". No personal effects were returned. None remained.

It had been a painful year for May. She had spent almost all of it without her husband. She had lost her mother. Then her husband. But she still had their child, little James. Now, just over a year old. And she had her widower father to care for. In the house with the shop and the stables.

***

On Thursday 17 August, little James was playing with some older children in the stable yard. Someone had made a swing out of rope. May had spent the late afternoon clearing empty cardboard boxes out of the shop and piling them in the yard. It was a perfect place for the children to play.

Arthur, May's father, came home at about 8 pm. It had been a long day, taking advantage of the light evenings on one of his building sites.

He herded the children away from the boxes, piled them up and set fire to them. He watched the fire catch then turned away and started to unfasten the rope the children had been playing with. He heard a scream. He turned round. The children were standing close to the burning boxes. Little James was leaning forward with his hands in the flames. Arthur pulled him away and put out the fire.

May rushed her son to a local doctor. He dressed the toddler's wounds. But the boy was still in pain. Late at night, she took him to the infirmary where his dressings were changed. The burns were not extensive but they hurt.

May took him to the Infirmary twice more the following day, Friday 18 August. Then again on the morning of Saturday 19 August. He was still crying with pain.

While they were waiting in the Outpatients Department, he had a fit. They called the house surgeon. He suspected tetanus and admitted Little James, intending to begin treatment for his infection. Perhaps using the newly discovered serum therapy.

They put the toddler to bed but the fits would not subside. It was too late for any treatment.

A final fit quietened him. An hour later, his heart stopped.

Printed in Great Britain
by Amazon.co.uk, Ltd.,
Marston Gate.